The Franco-Prussian War

A Captivating Guide to the War of 1870 between the French Empire and German States and the Role Otto von Bismarck Played in the Unification of Germany

Free Bonus from Captivating History
(Available for a Limited time)

Hi History Lovers!

Now you have a chance to join our exclusive history list so you can get your first history ebook for free as well as discounts and a potential to get more history books for free! Simply visit the link below to join.

Captivatinghistory.com/ebook

Also, make sure to follow us on Facebook, Twitter and Youtube by searching for Captivating History.

Contents

Introduction

When talking about 19th-century European history, the spotlight is often directed at Napoleon Bonaparte and his wars in the early 1800s. The rest of the century is somehow lumped together, peppered with stories of industrial developments and social and cultural evolutions. It was almost as if this period of time was a breather before the Great War of 1914. Such an approach has its merits, as indeed the 19th century was largely shaped by the changes in technology due to the Industrial Revolution and by new ways of thinking, which were brought about by the French Revolution and Napoleon. However, an important note in European history that deserves to be noticed and talked about is the Franco-Prussian War of 1870.

The war itself was short, lasting barely six months. Despite that, it managed to shake the foundations of Europe. It showcased French weakness and the rising industrialization and modernization of Prussia. In a way, this conflict threw a wrench in the perceived balance of power after Napoleon's defeat. Not only that, but it led to the creation of the unified German Empire under the iron fist of Chancellor Bismarck. As such, unified Germany immediately became a political, economic, and military powerhouse in continental Europe, lagging only behind the British Empire. On the other hand, it led to the fall of the last monarchical regime in France. Furthermore, it showcased the importance of utilizing modernizations in technology and bureaucracy within the army, as the Prussian military model became a forerunner of the changes that were to come.

Yet, the outcomes and effects of the war, on their own, could still be deemed somewhat less significant, especially if one is not interested in military history. However, when combined together, it could be seen as the first major step toward the "war to end all wars," both in the form of the great game of national politics but also in transformations on the battlefield. As such, the Franco-Prussian War rippled across history, rightfully calling out for our attention in our quest to better understand our shared past.

Chapter 1 – A Long Road to War: A Short History of Franco-German Relations

Usually, the story of the Franco-Prussian War would begin in the decade prior to it, most notably due to Bismarck's ascendance to the position of Prussian chancellor. However, while such an introduction suffices for understanding the immediate causes of the war, to fully grasp the larger historical framework, it would be better to begin in the Middle Ages.

Most people know that in the early 9th century, Charlemagne the Great extended the Frankish Empire to cover modern-day France, Germany, the Low Countries, Switzerland, parts of northern Italy, and Austria, as well as parts of the Balkans, Hungary, the Czech Republic, and Spain. The pope crowned him as the Holy Roman emperor in 800. However, after Charlemagne's death, his heirs were unable to agree upon the succession to the throne. By the mid-9th century, the former empire had been split into three sections after a civil war among his grandsons. After the Treaty of Verdun in 843, Charlemagne's grandsons formed West Francia (the core of future France), East Francia (the core of future Germany), and Middle

Francia (situated between them, including the Low Countries and parts of northern Italy) under a provisional unity. Such a fragile state quickly dissolved. Middle Francia was the most brittle, as it lacked any sort of geographical or demographic unity, and by the end of the century, it had fractured. Meanwhile, East and West Francia began competing for parts of its territories, most notably the provinces today known as Alsace and Lorraine.

Map of the Frankish Empire division into what was to become Germany and France.
Source: *https://commons.wikimedia.org/wiki/File:843-870_Europe.jpg*

Over the course of the next couple of centuries, two remaining Frankish states evolved into the more recognizable forms of France and Germany. In East Francia, that transformation came somewhat sooner, as, by the early 10th century, there was a growing idea that the kingdom belonged to the Germanic people, as it consisted of several Germanic tribes and peoples, like, for example, Frisians, Thuringii, and Saxons. Without delving too much into the formation of national identity, by the early 11th century, the official title of King of the Germans was in place. However, even prior to that, Otto I, a Germanic king of East Francia who was not a descendant of

Charlemagne, managed to revive the Holy Roman Empire in 962. Thus, German history became more closely linked with the imperial legacy, especially as by the late 15th century, it became known as the Holy Roman Empire of the German Nations. Regardless of the name, it is vital to mention that the Holy Roman Empire after 962 was an elective monarchy, where several princes and dukes elected their sovereign after the passing of the ruler. Therefore, this empire was also a confederacy of sorts, as it legally recognized the constituent states had a degree of independence beneath the imperial crown.

In contrast, West Francia's transformation into France was more direct and easily understandable. For several centuries, its rulers held the title King of the Franks, indicating they were the rulers of said people. However, by the early 12th century, a new trend among the rulers was to present themselves as sovereigns of lands, not people. Thus, East Francia's rulers started to adopt the title King of France, indicating they ruled the Frankish territories. Over the years, the Franks became the French, while their nation became France. Such phrasing was solidified by the early 13th century. Another contrast between France and Germany is that the former remained a kingdom, though many have questioned the idea of how Germany was exactly the Holy Roman Empire. Yet, throughout the medieval period, the French kingdom was quite decentralized, as local lords had a lot of freedom in respect to their sovereign. Thus, like in the German Empire in the east, the strength of a king's rule depended on his own competence.

In a rather simplified story of these two nations, their trajectories were rather different. Beginning in the 12th century, the French kings began to reaffirm their rule over the country, slowly centralizing their power. With many ups and downs, they slowly transformed their kingdom from a feudal monarchy to an absolute monarchy by the 16th century. With that also came a more unified national feeling, as the French gradually began identifying more with their country than with their local identities. In contrast, the Holy Roman Empire, as a nation, weakened. Local dukes, kings, and princes grew in strength. In turn, though the population of the Germanic constituent states saw their common ancestry, their identities weren't as closely knit as among the French. Despite that, the Holy Roman Empire remained an important political factor. From the mid-15th century onward, it was almost continuously ruled by the Habsburg dynasty, despite the official electoral system still being in place.

With that, the Holy Roman Empire became part of a much larger conglomerate that is today sometimes referred to as the Habsburg monarchy. At its greatest extent, in the early 16th century, this Habsburgian political entity, in addition to the Holy Roman Empire, covered modern-day Austria, Hungary, parts of Poland, the Czech Republic, Slovakia, Slovenia, Croatia, Spain, Portugal, and their colonial empires across the globe. As such, the Habsburg monarchy, and with it, the Holy Roman Empire, became one of the main competitors of France. This relationship is comparable to the better-known Anglo-French relations. However, while the Habsburg Empire remained strong, Germany proper continued to wane. The Habsburgs centered their rule in Austria, while the rest of the Holy Roman Empire continued to fracture into smaller and weaker duchies and provinces. Their former glory was finally trampled when Germany became Europe's battlefield during the Thirty Years' War (1618-1648). By then, the Holy Roman Empire as a country was factually almost nonexistent, a mere shell of its former glory. Regardless, its title was still a source of prestige for the Habsburgs.

The 17th century saw the Kingdom of France at one of its highest points, most notably during the reign of the famous Louis XIV (r. 1643-1715), while Germany was a unified entity solely on paper. Nonetheless, the two collided on several occasions, as the Habsburgs waged war with the French over their influence of continental Europe, for example, the Nine Years' War (1688-1697) or the War of the Spanish Succession (1701-1714). Overall, France aimed at expanding its power and domain in Europe. As such, it saw a weak Germany as a favorable eastern neighbor, as it meant a less immediate threat from the Habsburgs and less opposition in general. Furthermore, it also meant a possible route for eastward expansion, as exhibited with frequent struggles to gain control over the Alsace and Lorraine provinces. As a result of numerous wars throughout the 17th and 18th centuries, these two regions were often swapped between the French and the Habsburgs.

After the death of Louis XIV, France began its downward trajectory, as his heirs proved somewhat less competent and lost some costly wars. Most notable was the Seven Years' War (1756–1763), which France waged primarily against the British. However, the start of this war proved to be a turning point in Franco-German relations. During this conflict, France actually allied with the Habsburgs, while Prussia, a rising Germanic state in the east, sided with the British. The origins of Prussia can be traced to the Teutonic knights establishing their domain centered around Königsberg (modern-day Kaliningrad) on the shores of the Baltic Sea. For most of its history, it was just one of many duchies in the region, subjugated either to the Holy Roman Empire or the Kingdom of Poland. Its rise to power came during the 17th century, with the first step coming in 1619 when it passed into the hands of the Hohenzollern dynasty.

This was important because the Hohenzollerns held other estates in Germany, most notably Brandenburg and its capital of Berlin, while Prussia was officially a Polish fiefdom. Seeing the destruction caused by the Thirty Years' War inspired the Prussians to reform and strengthen their military and economy. Then, in 1657, the Duchy of Prussia gained its independence from the Polish Crown, giving free rein to the Hohenzollerns, at least in that region. As they continued to grow in strength, the rulers of Brandenburg-Prussia used the legal independence of Prussia to proclaim themselves kings in 1701. At that moment, King Frederick I of Prussia managed to convince Habsburg Emperor Leopold I to confirm his title, though it was phrased "king in Prussia" rather than "king of Prussia," as Leopold wanted it to be clear that the rest of Frederick's domain still lay under imperial rule. Over the next several decades, Prussia, which began shedding the Brandenburg part of its name, continued to expand its military might. This was best encapsulated by a late 18th-century French politician who said, "Prussia is not a state with an army, but an army with a state."

By the 1740s, the Prussians were powerful enough to directly challenge the Habsburgs. Under the energetic leadership of Frederick II (also known as Frederick the Great; r.1740–1786), they waged two short wars against Habsburgian domains, which were a part of the larger European conflict known as the War of the Austrian Succession (1740–1748). During that confrontation, the Prussians allied with the French, while the Habsburgs were aided by the British, with several other minor allies on both sides. For the first time, Prussia showcased its power, securing several victories and a major expansion by conquering the rich province of Silesia, a region in what is today southwestern Poland. When the Seven Years' War came, the alliances changed. Prussia sided with the British, while the Habsburg monarchy partnered with their former bitter enemy France. Such reversal of roles highlights a significant change in Franco-German relations. From then on, Prussia was the dominant German state, now colliding with France for dominance in Europe. Furthermore, the Habsburgs' grip over the Holy Roman Empire had weakened. They relied almost exclusively on their Austrian domain and, in part, on Bohemia (modern-day Czech Republic), while other Germanic states remained somewhat of an unorganized mess. They were only formally united as a single entity.

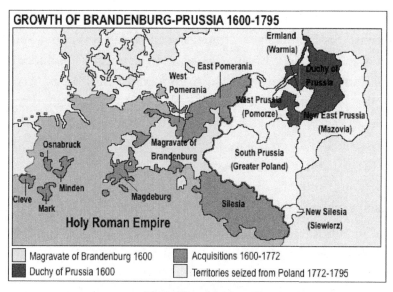

GROWTH OF BRANDENBURG-PRUSSIA 1600-1795

Ermland (Warmia)

East Pomerania

West Pomerania

West Prussia (Pomorze)

Duchy of Prussia

New East Prussia (Mazovia)

Osnabruck

Magravate of Brandenburg

South Prussia (Greater Poland)

Minden

Magdeburg

Cleve

Mark

Silesia

Holy Roman Empire

New Silesia (Siewierz)

Magravate of Brandenburg 1600
Duchy of Prussia 1600
Acquisitions 1600-1772
Territories seized from Poland 1772-1795

Map of Prussian expansion
Source: Attribution-ShareAlike 3.0 Unported (CC BY-SA 3.0)
https://commons.wikimedia.org/wiki/File:Acprussiamap2.gif

Portrait of King Frederick II
Source: https://en.wikipedia.org/wiki/File:Friedrich_Zweite_Alt.jpg

The final years of the 18th century once again exhibited that France and Germany, or in this case Prussia, were linked as opposites. While France remained on a downward spiral, with internal social issues tearing up the country, Prussia continued to rise. During the 1770s, it took part in the First Partition of Poland, together with Russia and the Habsburgs, most notably accruing so-called West Prussia on the Baltic coast. With that, Prussia managed to connect its Brandenburg provinces with Prussia proper. The Second and Third Partitions came during the 1790s, during which time Poland lost all of its territories. However, Prussia gained control over the Podlachia and Masovia provinces, including Warsaw, which was south of Prussia proper. While the Kingdom of Prussia was expanding, the French monarchy crumbled in 1789 due to the eruption of the French Revolution, culminating with the formation of the First French Republic in 1792.

The French Revolution and the treatment of Louis XVI prompted both the Habsburgs and Prussia to react, issuing threats to the revolutionaries. Such a response was to be expected, as the spreading of revolutionary ideas was a threat to all crowned heads in Europe. France's retort to the threat was a declaration of war. Over the next three years, the war raged on with shifting fortunes, while the list of French enemies grew, eventually including Spain, Portugal, and Britain. However, by 1795, Prussia had enough of the costly war that brought no gains. Thus, a separate peace was signed, allowing it to focus on the Third Partition of Poland. The Habsburgs forged on, this time allied with the British. The major zones of confrontations were northern Italy and the lands of the Holy Roman Empire. After several more years of struggles, both the Habsburgs (1801) and Britain (1802) asked for peace, while France emerged as the victor from the decade-long war. Yet, the ultimate result of the French Revolutionary Wars was the rise of Napoleon, as he seized control over the republic in 1799 through a coup.

Napoleon's rise brought a change to French policies, both internal and external. On the one hand, Napoleon quickly showed his autocratic tendencies, slowly working his way to becoming an emperor in 1804. Nevertheless, France officially retained the title of a republic, as the nation was dubbed a republic until 1809. More importantly, Napoleon was an ambitious and capable commander. His grandiose plans included an expansion of French power; thus, the wars he waged were no longer defensive ones, as they had been in the times of the French Revolution. He led France into a European-wide offensive. In their efforts to contain him, other European powers formed a coalition against France in 1803, with Britain, Russia, the Habsburgs, Naples, and Sweden as members. While Britain had some success on the seas, with a notable win at Trafalgar (1805), the continental war was going in Napoleon's favor. Most notable was his victory over joint Russian and Austrian troops at Austerlitz (1805). Not only did this force the Habsburgs to withdraw from the alliance and seek a separate peace, but this was also the moment the Holy Roman Empire began its final fall.

First, in July 1806, Napoleon signed separate treaties with sixteen Germanic states that were part of the empire. They formally withdrew from the Holy Roman Empire and formed the Confederation of the Rhine. The Habsburgs weren't pleased, but Napoleon's ultimatum led Emperor Francis II to proclaim the final dissolution of the Holy Roman Empire in August 1806, ending almost a millennium-long history of that state. Francis became the emperor of Austria, while other smaller Germanic states flocked to the confederation. Napoleon created it mainly as a military alliance and a buffer to the eastern enemies of France. It signaled a major transgression of French power over Germany, as France penetrated deeper into Germanic lands than ever before. It was especially shocking for the Prussians, who had remained outside the confederation, as now France contested their leadership among the Germans.

Painting of Napoleon
Source: https://commons.wikimedia.org/wiki/File:Napoleon_in_1806.PNG

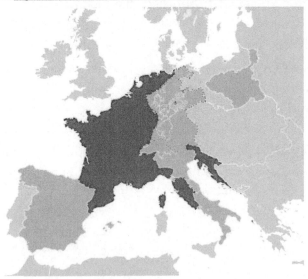

Map of the French Empire and its satellite states in 1812, including the newly formed Confederation of the Rhine
Source: TRAJAN 117 This W3C-unspecified vector image was created with Inkscape ., CC BY-SA 3.0 <https://creativecommons.org/licenses/by-sa/3.0>, via Wikimedia Commons https://commons.wikimedia.org/wiki/File:French_Empire_(1812).svg

The Napoleonic Wars continued over the next several years, with Prussia and Austria attempting to challenge France on several occasions. Yet, they were defeated multiple times, losing parts of their territories as a result. The French took western parts of Prussia and formed the Kingdom of Westphalia, while Austria lost Carinthia, Carniola, its Adriatic ports, and Galicia. Some of those went under direct French rule, while other territories were ceded to French allies in Germany. Nonetheless, Napoleon's rule began to chafe the local Germans, while the continued struggle against the French continued to shape the shared Germanic identity among the population. It mattered little that many Germans were on opposite sides of the battlefield. As the French power began to stretch thin and began to suffer losses, Napoleon's Germanic allies started to abandon him. After the so-called Battle of the Nations (1813), many left the confederation, and it crumbled without French support. Soon, Napoleon suffered his final defeats in 1814 and 1815. Europe was finally at peace.

The future of Europe was decided in the Congress of Vienna (1815). There, all major nations, including the defeated France, now ruled by the old Bourbon dynasty, came together to hammer out the European political landscape after Napoleon's defeat. Of course, France lost most of its expansive gains, while many nations were created and incorporated into other nations. For example, a shortly revived Duchy of Warsaw (Poland) was once again divided between Russia and Prussia. More importantly for the tale of Franco-Germanic relations was the fate of the region that was once the Holy Roman Empire. Prussia regained its lost territories while also receiving Swedish Pomerania, Saxony, and the city of Danzig. The Habsburgs mostly regained their lost lands. Other minor German states had their territorial gains under Napoleon officially recognized. Yet, perhaps most important was the fact that the Holy Roman Empire wasn't revived. Instead, a new German Confederation was formed, covering most of the former Holy Roman Empire. It was comprised of more than forty independent entities in a loose alliance under Austrian guidance.

From then on, two major things influenced the further development of the German nation. Due to the spurred nationalistic feelings, the idea of German unification began to spread across the Germanic states, or at least among their elites. This was intertwined with the growing competition between Prussia and Austria for the leadership role of the Germanic world. The Prussians were eager to utilize the rise of these nationalistic ideas of unification, while the Austrians opposed it. The Habsburgs realized that Austrian integration into a purely Germanic state was largely incompatible with their empire, which was compromised of numerous European nations, like Hungarians, Czechs, Serbs, and Croats. On the other hand, the Prussians felt that unification could be done under their leadership. The first step they made was the creation of a customs union (the Zollverein) in 1818. It was a commercial alliance that helped the growth of German and Prussian industries and economy. By the mid-1830s, it encompassed most of the Germanic states, but the Prussians were careful to exclude the Austrians from it.

Lifting the trade barriers did more than just strengthen the economic expansion of the Germanic states, which began rapid industrialization in the 1840s. It also further facilitated the growing feeling of a shared German identity. All the while, France went through a period of ups and downs. Its economy and power rose but not as fast as in the Germanic states, while its political and social life was unstable, to say the least. In 1830, a coup led to a change on the throne. King Charles X was replaced by Louis Philippe, a member of a Bourbon dynasty side-branch. This change came as a response to the unwavering autocracy of Charles. Thus, Louis was supposed to be a "citizen king," whose power rested on the bourgeoisie. This change was evident by the fact that his title was "King of the French," not of France. The French monarchy was certainly feeling the repercussions of the revolution.

However, as time went by, this "citizen king" also turned toward authoritarianism to preserve his reign, leading France into further turmoil. It exploded in 1848, as the workers and lower classes remained unsatisfied with the regime. With a new revolution, the monarchy was once again overthrown, and the Second Republic was formed. By the end of the year, Louis Napoleon Bonaparte, Napoleon's nephew, emerged as its president and leader of "all the people." While France was going through yet another revolution and internal upheaval, this time, the rebellious sentiment bubbled over to other nations as well. As such, it became known as the Springtime of Nations or the Revolutions of 1848, as people across the world rebelled. Both Prussia and Austria were affected but in very different ways.

The Prussians rebelled against the absolute monarchy of King Friedrich Wilhelm IV (Frederick William; r. 1840–1861), leading to some concessions on his part. Despite that, there were major demonstrations and even casualties. Around Prussia and among other minor Germanic states, most protests and uprisings were actually aimed at promoting German unification alongside demands for liberal reforms, as it was seen as the logical next step toward a better life. This caused a crisis for the German Confederation, as many wanted more direct elections and participation. The upheaval culminated with a new National Assembly, which directly offered King Friedrich the crown of a united Germany. He refused, as it was too radical a step for him. By late 1849, the revolutionary tide in Germany was broken by local princes and dukes, often through immense violence. Nevertheless, the signaled support for German unity didn't go unnoticed.

An 1850 map of Europe.
Source: https://commons.wikimedia.org/wiki/File:1850_Mitchell_Map_of_Europe_-_Geographicus_-_Europe-mitchell-1850.jpg

Farther south, the Austrian Habsburgs were faced with more ominous threats, as pretty much all non-Germanic nationalities under their rule revolted, asking for more autonomy. The crisis was so strong that Emperor Ferdinand I abdicated in favor of his more liberal nephew, Franz Joseph. Even worse, the empire was embroiled in a conflict that resembled a civil war, as the various rebellions and nationalities clashed against each other, sometimes even in favor of the Habsburgs, as the people hoped to gain some favor. In the end, peace was restored, yet the Austrians were still too preoccupied with domestic affairs to influence the affairs of the German Confederation to any significant degree. As the dust continued to settle, most of the Germanic states, including Prussia and Austria, returned to their conservative ways since the results of the uprisings proved fleeting. At the same time, the Austro-Prussian rivalry was reheating once again.

The French Republic went through a similar path. Louis Napoleon Bonaparte quietly and steadily regrouped his positions and power, with the country slowly descending into a new autocracy. By 1852, he decided to "promote" himself from president to emperor, becoming known as Emperor Napoleon III, once again transforming the republic into an empire. This transformation went largely unchallenged. With this move, France was once more looking to prove its dominant position in Europe. The revival of such imperial politics sent France on a collision course with Prussia, which continued its rise as a European power and the center of German unification.

Chapter 2 – Enemies at the Borders: Immediate Causes for the War

While there were enmities between the French and the Germans, intertwined with their long-running struggle for dominance over continental Europe, those were not the immediate causes for the war between France and Prussia. They did facilitate it, in a long line of cause and effect, but the direct origin of the conflict began to arise only during the 1850s.

By 1852, Napoleon III had established himself as the new French emperor, and he was filled with dreams of grandeur. During his reign, especially in the early years, France exhibited internal stability with signs of economic growth and gradual industrialization. Such a position allowed him to pursue his ideas of glory in foreign affairs. Napoleon III wanted to return France to the forefront of the world powers and gain the same kind of respect and prestige his uncle had. He had some success, as he expanded the French colonial domain in Indochina and Africa, strengthened French control over Algeria, and made a foothold in China, alongside other colonial powers. However, these successes seemed minor when compared with his failures in

Europe. During the Crimean War (1854–1856), he sided with the victorious British and Ottoman forces against Imperial Russia, yet that expedition yielded only expenses without any palpable gains. Then, in 1859, he turned his gaze closer to home, deciding to support the Italian Kingdom of Piedmont in their war to expel the Austrians from the Apennine Peninsula. His goal was to expand French influence over what he hoped to become a loose Italian confederation.

An 1855 portrait of Napoleon III
Source: https://commons.wikimedia.org/wiki/File:Franz_Xaver_Winterhalter_Napoleon_III.jpg

Depiction of the French presence in Algeria
Source: https://commons.wikimedia.org/wiki/File:Arrival_of_Marshal_Randon_in_Algier-Ernest-Francis_Vacherot_mg_5120.jpg

Initially, it seemed Napoleon's plans might succeed, as joint Italo-French forces won against the Habsburgs, prompting them to ask for peace within a few months. France gained some land in northern Italy, mainly around Milan. These were exchanged with Piedmont for areas around Nice and Savoy. Despite achieving territorial gains, Napoleon's plans quickly turned sour. After two years of conflicts and struggles, Piedmont expanded across the peninsula, leaving only the papacy in Rome and the Austrians in Venice. Instead of a loose confederation, by early 1861, France had gained a unified Kingdom of Italy as its southern neighbor. To make matters worse for Napoleon, he suffered further diplomatic failures in North America. His politics almost dragged France into the US Civil War (1861–1865), while his attempt to secure Mexico under French influence failed miserably. The expedition forces sent to secure a puppet ruler in 1861 fought against the Mexicans for six years before being defeated in 1867. The French ruler in Mexico was executed, France was humiliated, and Napoleon lost many of his supporters. Instead of bringing peace and prosperity, he brought wars that ended mostly in losses or empty victories and financial debacles. To make matters worse, his erratic foreign policy alienated most French allies, leaving her alone on the world stage.

While France seemed to be on a downward spiral, Prussia's fate appeared to follow a different trajectory. Although Napoleon III enjoyed a promising start, Friedrich Wilhelm IV led Prussia through a rocky period in the 1850s. He had to sort out political instability caused by the Revolutions of 1848 while continuing to expand the economy and industry. Prussian weakness, especially on the diplomatic front, was highlighted throughout the decade. First, it suffered a defeat against Denmark in the First Schleswig War (1848-1851), which was more the result of international pressure than its failures on the battlefield. Furthermore, other great powers marginalized Prussia during the Crimean War (1854-1856) and the Italian War (1859). With that, its status as a European power became an issue going into the 1860s.

Such developments didn't sit particularly well with Friedrich's younger brother, Wilhelm (William), who became a regent when the king suffered a stroke. His plan to return Prussian status to its former glory rested on expanding its military might. Wilhelm sprang into action in 1861 when he became the king after the death of his older brother. Such expenditures caused some backlash among the Prussian politicians. Amidst the crisis, King Wilhelm I considered abdicating but instead appointed Otto von Bismarck as the prime minister in September of 1862. This proved to a crucial turning point for Prussia. At the time, Bismarck wasn't a prominent or very experienced politician. His career was mostly in foreign affairs, serving first as the Prussian representative in the assembly of the German Confederation and then as an ambassador in Russia and France. Wilhelm chose him only after Minister of War Albrecht von Roon advised him to do so. Nevertheless, Bismarck quickly proved his worth, as he managed to outmaneuver opponents of the military reforms.

A perfect storm was formed in the political and military leadership of Prussia. King Wilhelm, an old general who believed that political power lay in the nation's military, was supported by Bismarck, who believed that Prussia's ultimate goal must be the unification of Germany through "blood and iron." Roon, believing in the necessity of military reforms, bridged the gap between politics and the army. Finally, the Prussian chief of staff was famous Field Marshal Helmuth von Moltke, who personally led the reorganization and restructuring of the Prussian forces. Moltke observed the advances of other European nations during the 1850s, realizing that the Prussian military had to expand in number, adopt new types of arms, master quicker and better mobilization, improve communication and deployment using modern technologies, and create a professional and well-trained officer core. By 1864, Prussia, under Bismarck's leadership, was prepared to showcase its newfound strength.

Its first opponent was Denmark, a perfect target to readdress Prussian frustration from the Schleswig War. A change on the Danish throne in 1863 opened up territorial disputes over the territories of Schleswig and Holstein, provinces that were populated mostly by Germans. They were officially part of the German Confederation but were under Danish reign. The new Danish monarch issued a new constitution, which proclaimed Schleswig as an integral part of the Danish Crown, violating the peace treaty from the 1850s. That gave Bismarck enough pretext to launch a campaign, utilizing German nationalist sentiment to further legitimize the Prussian attack. It was enough to bring the rest of the confederation, including the Austrians, to join in to defend the German people. More importantly, other major powers remained largely uninterested in the conflict, with only Britain showing mild support to the Danes. In the end, the combined forces of the German states outnumbered and outgunned the Danish forces, conquering almost all of Denmark by mid-1864. By October, a peace treaty had been signed. Austria gained Holstein, while Prussia gained Schleswig and recognition of its strength.

An 1857 photo of Wilhelm I
Source: *https://commons.wikimedia.org/wiki/File:Kaiser_Wilhelm_I_1857.jpg*

An 1860s illustration of Bismarck, Roon, and Moltke in said order
Source: *https://commons.wikimedia.org/wiki/File:BismarckRoonMoltke.jpg*

After the quick victory, Austria and Prussia agreed to form joint sovereignty over the two provinces, as they were historically seen as a single entity. Expectedly, this created numerous issues between the two nations, leading some historians to assume it was all done according to Bismarck's grand design. Such claims are debatable, to say the least, yet Bismarck's ability to adapt to new situations and use them to his and Prussia's advantage remains undisputed. By early 1866, tensions had risen enough for the Prussians to accuse the Austrians of breaching the joint sovereignty by allowing Holstein to organize an assembly. Mutual accusations were exchanged, leading both sides to look for allies. Bismarck secured an alliance with Italy, as it wanted to liberate Venice from the Habsburgs, while Austria found support from the other German states, which feared Prussian military might. Both sides began concentrating troops on the borders, issuing mobilization orders. War was clearly imminent.

Napoleon III was also interested in the development of the Austro-Prussian crisis. He met with Bismarck in late 1865, assuring him that France would stay neutral in the case of war. It seems that Napoleon believed that a conflict between the German states would only exhaust them, allowing him to gain political concessions for France and even enlarge it. However, neutrality was all that Bismarck and Prussia needed. By May 1866, both sides were geared up for war. In the early days of June, Austrians brought the issues to the assembly of the German Confederation while also preparing for the gathering of the Holstein Diet. The Prussians then proclaimed their agreement with Austria was void and invaded Holstein, while the German Confederation responded with a partial mobilization. Instead of intimidating them, this prompted the Prussians to declare that the German Confederation was dissolved. Their army invaded Saxony, Hesse, and Hanover, with Italy also declaring war on Austria.

Since the Prussian Army was reformed and modernized, it quickly dissolved any Austrian hopes of a swift victory and simultaneously crumbled all of Napoleon's plans. Prussia managed to defeat the Hanoverian forces by the end of June and also amassed troops near Moravia (modern-day Czech Republic), where the Austrians were gathering their forces. Two large armies met in the Battle of Königgrätz (present-day Sadová) on July 3rd. The Prussians exhibited technological and tactical supremacy, leaving the Austrian army running from the battlefield in shreds. While they continued to advance through the Czech Republic and Slovakia, other Prussian troops defeated Saxon and Bavarian troops. The Austrians, knowing they were facing total defeat, asked for peace on July 22nd, ending the war in a mere seven weeks. A few days later, on August 12th, the Italians were forced to end their campaign as well, though their struggle seemed a bit more even, as both sides achieved some victories.

After Moltke and the Prussian Army achieved victory on the battlefield, it was up to Bismarck to capitalize on it. In fact, he was in favor of accepting a quick defeat from the Austrians without pursuing further gains. As a keen politician and diplomat, Bismarck knew that if Prussia pushed too far, Russia or France might intervene. Furthermore, he wanted to avoid too much revanchism from Austria or other Germanic states. The peace was ratified in Prague in late August but not without French interference. Prussia annexed Schleswig, Holstein, Hanover, Hesse-Kassel, Nassau, and Frankfurt, while the rest of the northern Germanic states were organized into the North German Confederation. Through this confederation, Prussia basically controlled their military and foreign relations; these states were basically just a step away from annexation. In trying to prevent the further unification of Germanic states under Prussia, Napoleon demanded Bismarck's assurance of independence for Saxony, Bavaria, Württemberg, Baden, and Hesse-Darmstadt. By early October, Italy had managed to secure Venice, though it was first handed over to France, which then transferred it to Italy. This was done to save Austrian face, for they claimed to have won their war with Italy.

The Peace of Prague also meant that the Habsburgs were excluded from German affairs and matters of unification. The merger was to encompass only so-called Lesser Germany (*Kleindeutschland*), not Austria or any other Habsburgian lands. Despite that, France was still threatened. Instead of having a loose confederation that was exhausted by war, Napoleon was faced with the strong North German Confederation, which was basically an enlarged Prussia. It had a population of thirty million, compared to France's thirty-eight million, with a much more developed industry. Furthermore, due to military reforms, Prussia had an army roughly one-third larger than France. If Prussia was to spread to the southern Germanic states, below the River Mein, not only would it gain a substantial boost in population and the economy but also a strategic advantage against the French. Attacking on the wide front from Luxembourg to Switzerland would allow them to easily flank French defenses. Thus, preventing German unification became one of the paramount goals of Napoleon's politics.

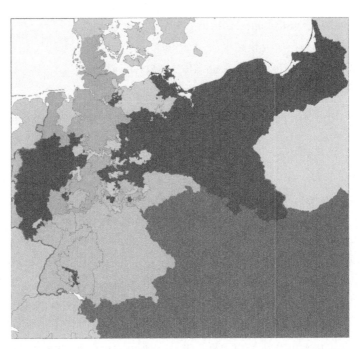

Map of the Austro-Prussian War of 1866—Austrian Empire (red), Austrian allies (pink), Prussian allies (light blue), Prussia (dark blue), Prussia acquisitions (cyan), and neutral states (green).

Soon after the dust had settled, Napoleon tried to buy Luxembourg, which was at the time under a personal union with the Netherlands, ruled by King William III. William was in debt, and Napoleon sought to improve both his position in France and France's position in Europe. An added bonus was that Luxembourg was a rather important strategic fortification between France and Prussia. Napoleon hoped that Bismarck wouldn't object to it, as it was supposedly part of their oral agreement made before the Austro-Prussian War. It seems that Bismarck hinted at having no objection to French hegemony in Belgium and Luxembourg if France remained neutral. However, by early 1867, Prussia was in a position to object to French expansion. All of a sudden, Bismarck stopped playing the role of Napoleon's malleable protégé concerned about French reactions. Instead, his political posturing was one of dominance and power, as he threatened with war if France went through with the purchase. Instead of war, a conference of major powers was held in London, with the final result being the independence of Luxembourg guaranteed by those nations.

Nevertheless, tensions remained high as both sides were on the brink of war. Yet, it seems that neither of them was prepared to stake their bets. Napoleon realized that France needed to modernize its military if it was to challenge the Prussians on the battlefield. Bismarck was concerned that another war might unify other major powers against Prussia, as they were sure to feel threatened by its rising power. Instead, he decided to bide his time while preparing the stage for a final reckoning with France. Using his keen political skills, Bismarck leaned on Napoleon's posturing. This made France seem more powerful than it was while also showing it as a possible threat due to its publicized interest in taking control of Belgium, Luxembourg, and even the Rhineland. In the eyes of the other powers, it started to look like France was a much bigger threat than the enlarged Prussia. Playing on that, Bismarck went on to work on isolating France from acquiring possible allies against Prussia.

In 1868, Bismarck once again taunted the French. He formed an all-German customs parliament, or *Zollparlament*, strengthening Prussian ties with the southern Germanic states. Of course, this irked Napoleon, and he reminded Prussia of his previous demands for the independence of those Germanic countries. He even prolonged summer military maneuvers in hopes of being taken more seriously. This worked for Bismarck. Once again, it was France that seemed threatening, as Prussia was far from able to absorb the southern states peacefully. Their rulers were keen on maintaining their sovereignty despite wanting an eased trade with Prussia. Napoleon's posturing was also working in favor for Bismarck internally. The possible French invasion only heated up German nationalistic feelings, which was especially important in the southern states. As time passed, despite the upper classes remaining adamant in retaining political independence, their citizens slowly began favoring a unified nation state. This was a reality that could only be attained through Prussia.

While the two nations remained in what could be described as a diplomatic stare-down, both Napoleon and Bismarck faced issues at home. The French, or at least the urban elite, began voicing their displeasure with the emperor's politics. They deplored his rather authoritarian constitution. The economy also began to show signs of distress. The expenses of Napoleon's various adventures, from Mexico to Italy, began to catch up, and even the latest military reforms demanded a substantial investment. Furthermore, his own extravagant lifestyle and leeching entourage worsened the emperor's image among the masses. In an attempt to secure his shaken rule, Napoleon called for an election in 1869, hoping his candidates would win through political trickery. However, even with ballot stuffing, gerrymandering, and other similar tactics, the opposition managed to secure 25 percent of the seats in the assembly. In reality, the opposition was much closer to 50 percent, prompting massive protests and demonstrations. Urban factory workers even began demanding a "red revolution" and a new republic. The emperor was prepared to use violence to break these efforts, but he instead chose a softer approach. Attempting to appease the protestors, he relaxed his authoritarian reign and put an eminent liberal reformer, Émile Ollivier, in the position of prime minister. Despite that, France remained rather divided and troubled. The only thing that all the French could agree upon was supporting the conflict with Prussia, as it was a matter of national pride.

On the other side of the border, Bismarck also ran into domestic troubles. In the Prussian assembly, he had to fight both the liberals, who wanted to reduce the size and expenditure of the military, and the conservatives, who opposed new laws and taxes. Furthermore, he had to wrestle with other Germanic governments and the confederation assembly. Making matters even worse, Bismarck also faced the issue of the rising industrial working class, which was permeated with socialist ideals. His goals of unification were additionally complicated by the fact that the southern Germanic states began leaning away from Prussia; they even began thinking about asking for French protection in the case of war. The northern states also began to question Prussian leadership to a degree. Bismarck's position was further shaken by numerous local national liberals who thought he was taking too much time to unify the states. While the elites and politicians were strung all over the political scale, the common population started to grow tired of the complicated system of overlapping assemblies and constant elections. Stagnation and discouragement began to spread when it came to matters of unification. Thus, while Napoleon favored war as a means of securing his reign, Bismarck saw the conflict as a crude tool that would remove rising obstacles to the German union.

The gunpowder kegs were aligned; all that was needed was a proper spark. The first one came in early 1870 when there was a rumor of the North German Confederation assembly offering King Wilhelm the title of Kaiser, or emperor. Both Wilhelm and Bismarck seemed in favor of such a development, yet Napoleon vocally threatened with war. In the end, the matter never moved further toward actualization. Soon afterward, another spark was deliberately set by Bismarck. He, or rather Prussia, invested in a railway through Switzerland, connecting Italy and the Germanic states. When such a subtle hint went unnoticed, Bismarck gave a well-measured speech. Without sounding aggressive or threatening, he hinted at an existence of a Prusso-Italian alliance aimed at France, which would be facilitated by said railway link. The French public once again cried for blood, yet the issue didn't evolve any further. Napoleon and his government remained surprisingly passive and inert. While Bismarck worked on isolating France, Napoleon's foreign minister just stood by watching. For example, by 1870, Italy no longer felt fidelity to Napoleon, despite France waging a costly war in 1859 on its behalf.

Realizing that his government needed more active and forceful diplomacy, Napoleon III appointed Duke Antoine Agénorde Gramont as his minister of foreign relations. Gramont saw himself as Bismarck's match, promising he would manufacture a conflict on whatever excuse arose first. He wanted to teach Prussia a lesson and dismantle its position that had been gained in 1866. Prime Minister Ollivier agreed, stating that the next disrespectful action from Bismarck and Prussia must lead to war. At the time, sixty-two-year-old Napoleon was ill and unable to involve himself more directly in the decision-making process, yet his appointed ministers were set on the warpath. Little did they know that they were walking straight into Bismarck's trap, one he had been preparing since September of 1869. The Spanish Parliament then offered their crown to Leopold Hohenzollern, Wilhelm's cousin. Besides recognizing the rise of Prussia through such a choice, Leopold had other benefits as well. He looked like a versatile and prestigious candidate.

Despite sounding like quite an offer, both Leopold and Wilhelm initially rejected it. Spain was unstable and in search of a new royal house since it had deposed the old Bourbon dynasty in 1868. If Leopold was to be chased off, it would bring shame to the entire Hohenzollern dynasty. However, Bismarck saw an opportunity there, and in May of 1870, he enticed Leopold's father to accept in his name. A few weeks later, Leopold himself agreed. By early July, the news had reached France, prompting an immediate fiery response. All of France was gearing up for war, for if the Spanish throne went to the Hohenzollerns, they would be encircled and their position weakened beyond repair. It seemed both Bismarck and Gramont would get their war. Yet, Wilhelm was worried that he'd seem like an instigator. Thus, without discussing it with his chancellor, he persuaded Leopold and his father to reject the offer, which they did on July 11th. It seemed that the crisis would be averted, which possibly seemed like a sign of weakness in Gramont's eyes.

Despite achieving a diplomatic victory, Gramont wasn't satisfied. Since he was denied an opportunity to settle the score through war, he wanted to humiliate the Prussians. It is also significant to note that he wasn't alone in the sentiment, as most of the French public and political elite seemed thirsty for war. Pushing his fortunes, Gramont sent a telegram to the French ambassador in Prussia, demanding a public and written renunciation from Wilhelm I, as well as a pledge that Prussia would never reach for the Spanish Crown. The ambassador met with the king on July 13th at Bad Ems, a spa, where Wilhelm was on a summer retreat. The Prussian king listened to the demand, then abruptly walked away without a word. He immediately sent a dispatch to Bismarck in Berlin. The message from Ems arrived while the chancellor was despondent about his plans crumbling. As he read about the events in Ems, Bismarck's calculated and unscrupulous political mind immediately saw an opportunity.

A later illustration of the Ems meeting between King Wilhelm I (left) and the French ambassador (right).
Source: https://commons.wikimedia.org/wiki/File:Bad_Ems_001.jpg

While keeping the original meaning of the message, Bismarck reworded part of it to sound as if the king was rude toward the ambassador, emphasizing that he refused him an audience after the initial talk. At the same time, he stressed that the French demand was insulting to Wilhelm. Then he circulated the message through newspapers across Europe. For Bismarck's plan to work, he needed France to make the first move. The so-called Ems Dispatch became the perfect red flag for the "Gallic bull." The undiplomatic wording of the meeting between the ambassador and the king was publicized on July 14th, adding insult to injury as it was Bastille Day, a national holiday in France. For Gramont and the agitated French, it was a gauntlet across the face. By the next day, France had ordered mobilization, followed by the Prussians and other Germanic states. After a few days spent in serving bureaucratic necessities, on July 19th, France declared war on Prussia. Finally, both Bismarck and Gramont got the war for which they yearned.

In the end, on the grand scale of things, the Franco-Prussian War began because of the long-lasting competition between the French and the Germans, as the European balance of power was tipping. One side wanted to retain its superiority, while the other wanted to become the dominant power. A pinnacle of that struggle was the issue of German unification, which was undoubtedly a tilting moment in history. However, when seen from a more immediate and closer historical perspective, it was a war that was sparked by the political needs of leaders in both France and Prussia. Both nations had internal issues and fractures that a war could mend through the power of unifying nationalism. Finally, the war was avoidable, especially when considering that the final crisis that ignited the gunpowder keg was quite frivolous on its own.

Chapter 3 – Two Fighters in the Ring: Prussian and French Armies, Tactics, and Organization

To understand the course of the war, we must first get acquainted with the state of both the French and the Prussian forces. The most common depiction is one of Prussian superiority, where the Germans were professional soldiers equipped with modern weaponry, while the French were a ragtag mass waging war with outdated guns. The reality is, of course, much more complicated than that.

The first issue that needs to be addressed is the matter of numbers, showcasing the first of several major differences between the two warring sides. On one side was France, which had a larger standing army, roughly 400,000 strong. The proposed reforms were supposed to swell that number up to roughly 800,000, but they were incomplete by 1870. Thus, on the brink of the war, the French headquarters counted on about 500,000 men, who were conscripted in about three weeks. Furthermore, the proposed reforms were supposed to form local militia units named *Garde Mobile*, a territorial defense made up of non-drafted able-bodied men who would have some limited military training. These troops weren't ready at all in 1870, numbering only about 100,000 conscripts, and their fighting capabilities and deployment speed were questionable at best.

The Prussians, or to be more precise, the North German Federation as a whole, had a smaller standing army, around 300,000 strong. However, it had a much deeper well of reserves and their own militia, the *Landwehr*, which would increase its fighting strength to just shy of one million men. Furthermore, the south Germanic states could field another 200,000. However, the Prussian high command believed their southern allies might not join in, despite secret military agreements that had been signed in the years prior to the war. The discrepancies in the strength of the two warring sides are mostly accountable by the different organizations and drafting systems of the armies, with Prussia favoring wider conscription. Yet, it is also vital to mention that by the second half of the 19th century, France was becoming an older nation with a lower reproduction rate. This meant that every generation would produce fewer soldiers than the one before. Regardless, it was clear that the Germans had numerical superiority, at least on paper, yet those numbers in the end also depended upon the speed of mobilization and deployment.

When seeing these rough numbers, common sense dictates that the French should have been more worried about their position on the battlefield. This wasn't so, mostly due to the slight hubris of the commanding officers. Many of them reckoned that the French were more professional, as the conscripted soldiers served at least seven years and were given incentives for reenlisting. Thus, by 1870, roughly half of the French soldiers had been in active service for more than seven years. In comparison, the Prussian soldiers had three years of active duty, followed by four years as reserves, and then another five in the *Landwehr*. Thus, at least on paper, the French were professionals, while the Prussian Army was one of reservists. However, the reality was vastly different. According to accounts left by some French officers, instead of having professional and experienced troops, they often had men in their fifties or sixties, men who were jaded and cynical and often more focused on drinking in the barracks than on practicing their military skills. To make matters worse, when a fresh batch of recruits came along, they often got dragged into the ways of their elders and quickly lost their vigor.

Prussian soldiers on a march in autumn of 1870.
Source:
https://commons.wikimedia.org/wiki/File:Troupes_allemandes_%C3%A0_Torcy_en_septembre_1870.jpg

In contrast, the Prussian Army seemed more fit and better trained, at least in theory. During their three years of primary service, they would undergo severe physical training, coupled with numerous theoretical lectures and stories of veterans. Furthermore, it has been said that the Prussians did more target practice shooting than any other army in Europe. Yet, the training wasn't only focused on military skills and knowledge. The officers, pretty much the only professional soldiers in the army, also worked on instilling their men with ethics, discipline, and morals, promoting the spirit of defending the fatherland. At first glance, it would seem that the Prussians were more than superior in this regard, yet their system did have substantial drawbacks. Despite their ferocious training, by 1870, not many of their troops ever witnessed actual combat, even in the reserves. Most of the French soldiers took part in at least one campaign. Moreover, they too had a desire to teach the Germans a lesson, which gave them ample fighting spirits, at least in the barracks.

There was also another jarring difference between the two armies in terms of their education. The French tended to demean their foes, calling the Prussians an "army of lawyers." Despite their intentions to insult, this illustrates the fact that most Prussian soldiers had some form of basic education and literacy, thanks to compulsory primary schools. It allowed them to have a much better comprehension of maps and complicated tactical maneuvers, among other things. Like in everyday life, having an education meant having an easier understanding of what was going on. On the other hand, most of the French soldiers were uncultured and illiterate. This was partially caused by the lack of compulsory education but also due to how the draft system functioned. Unlike Germany, which pretty much made every able-bodied man enlist, the French drew a lottery every year. However, it was possible to buy out the enlistment for only 2,400 francs, something a bourgeois elite could easily pay. Even poor peasant families were sometimes able to scrape that amount up to keep their men at home. Nevertheless, with the upper classes pretty much avoiding the service, much of the French Army was made up of uneducated rural folk.

The level of education posed another problem for the French military at the time, as the majority of officers were drawn from conscription. The low wages and pensions offered little incentive even for the middle classes, let alone the elites. Thus, the same societal dregs that made up the recruits eventually made it to the officer's ranks, at least the junior ones. Their lack of education made them perfect for executing orders but not too viable for thinking on their own and assuming responsibility for the command over their troops. Even worse, the pace of advancing in the French Army was slow, sometimes taking a whole decade to earn a rank, leaving many of the junior officers in their fifties or even sixties. Such a system, altogether, provided lower-ranked officers who were often intellectually blank, physically unfit, and plagued with apathy and inertia. According to a French contemporary, they were best at keeping their mouths shut and getting numb in a tavern or café. This, of course, wasn't the case with the higher ranks, which consisted of educated elites, but they were instead beset by petty rivalries, jealousy, and favoritism.

Their Prussian counterparts, when it comes to the senior ranked officers, often shared those erosive traits as well. It was seemingly unavoidable, as these men were proud members of the elites whose egos were large enough to fill a room. However, unlike the French, who did little to deal with such faulty personalities, Moltke actively combated it through reassignments or outright dismissals. His commanders had to be cooperative at least to a minimum degree. Yet, the true difference in the officer corps was more striking in the lower ranks. The Prussian officers were often drawn from middle-class recruits, thus often having more than just basic education, and they were enticed to pursue their military careers through a much quicker advancement through the ranks. This meant Prussian junior officers were often much younger, fit, and more capable than their French counterparts. To further convince them to stay in the army, those officers were offered government sinecure as well as hefty pensions after retiring from the army. Nevertheless, their active wages remained mediocre.

A picture of Moltke circa 1870
Source:
https://commons.wikimedia.org/wiki/File:Helmuth_Karl_Bernhard_von_Moltke,_Count_von_Moltke_by_Carl_G%C3%BCnther_circa_1870.png

An illustration of Prussian officers honing their skills through wargames
Source: https://commons.wikimedia.org/wiki/File:Joseph_Nash_Kriegsspiel.png

These differences also created a contrast in the organizational aspect of the two armies. Over the course of the 19th century, Prussians created a rather systemic and hierarchical organization of their troops, which differed only slightly between peacetime and war. This was epitomized in the famed *Generalstab*, or Great General Staff, a full-time body that actively worked on maintaining a high degree of preparation, creating plans both for campaigns and mobilizations, and honing military tactics and skills through exercises like wargames. This created a constant baseline in the Prussian Army, making it ready for any contingency. The quality of the Great General Staff was only heightened by the fact that its members were picked solely based on merit and capabilities, ignoring seniority or connections. Members of this highest military body all trained together and learned the same military philosophy, which, at the time, was based on Moltke's vision of the army. This made them interchangeable and reliable. Such training also created a sense of comradery between them. Overall, the *Generalstab* was, as Moltke himself described it, a nervous system of the Prussian military, creating a strong administrative backbone and increasing its functionality.

On the other hand, the French military was much less organized, without an active staff during peacetime. While there was no active conflict, the army organization existed almost entirely on a regimental scale, tasked with creating group morale in a unit. And while the Germans practiced territorial placement of their units and recruits, the French distributed their soldiers without regard to their origins. Above them was a loose organization of various committees and guidelines, with the Ministry of War at its helm. It is worth noting that the French Army was nominally led by Emperor Napoleon III himself, contrasting Moltke's professionalism as the Chief of Staff in Prussia. As it was previously mentioned, while the Prussian command depended upon promoting capable officers, the French high command was a seniority-ridden organization. Thus, overall, the French Army was much more centralized and conservative, steeped in the traditions of the olden days. Some strides toward rectifying this were made in the years prior to the war, with an attempt to create territorial divisions of the army and making promotions based on the emperor's choices. Yet, these military reforms were either not finished or were completely scrapped by the early 1870s.

So far, the description of the two armies leans toward depicting the Prussians as the superior military force. However, it is important to note that the differences may not have been as stark as they might seem at first glance. Up to that point, the French were seen as the primary land force in Europe, with the British commanding the seas. They had a long tradition and showed their worth in numerous wars in the past. For many, they were indeed the favorite in a conflict that seemed inevitable in the eyes of many neutral observers. Furthermore, the balance of power may have tipped the other way if the planned military reforms in France had enough time to be fulfilled. Nevertheless, the French military had a few aces up its sleeves in terms of modern weaponry.

With the outbreak of the war, the main Prussian weapon was the Dreyse needle gun, a breechloading bolt action rifle. It was first introduced in the Prussian Army as far back as 1841, and it performed rather impressively. It had an estimated firing speed of 5 to 6 rounds per minute and an effective range of about 400 to 600 yards (365 to550 meters), while its maximum range went up to 750 yards (685 meters). It outperformed almost all other guns in use, proving its worth during the war with Denmark and the Habsburgs, who, at the time, still outfitted their troops with muzzle-loading rifles. Its major point of supremacy was its reload speed, as a Prussian soldier fired up to five shots while the Austrian managed to reload his gun once. However, it had several critical issues as well. Its range was far from desirable, and its breech mechanism wasn't perfectly fitted, making the gun lose vital firing pressure, which, in turn, made its shot far less powerful. It was said the Dreyse often inflicted lighter wounds; sometimes, casualties would even get back on their feet and continue fighting.

Prior to 1866, the French military used a muzzle-loading rifle similar to the Austrians. Yet, upon seeing how superior the Dreyse was, they decided to rush the development of a new gun: the Chassepot *Fusil modèle 1866*. Its design was finalized in late 1866 and introduced into service in 1867. The Chassepot was a superior rifle in all aspects. Its effective range was about 1,000 yards (915 meters), with its maximum range reportedly going up to 1,600 yards (1,465 meters). The rate of fire ranged between eight and fifteen rounds per minute. The Chassepot's breechloading mechanism was fitted with rubber seals, making it much more energy efficient. Its caliber was slightly smaller, 11 millimeters (0.433 inches) to 15.4 millimeters (0.61 inches); however, the French bullets were milled and jacketed in linen instead of paper and were also packed with more gunpowder. All of these smaller advantages amounted to higher muzzle velocity, longer range, better precision, and, most impressively, high stopping power. According to pre-war French testing, while the entry wound was still the size of a single bullet, exit wounds were usually seven to thirteen times larger. They caused massive damage to inner organs, bones, and muscle, making every hit a potentially deadly one. If that alone wasn't enough, the Chassepot was slightly shorter and lighter, making it easier for transport and use. Furthermore, its smaller caliber meant that the French soldiers could carry more ammunition than their Prussian counterpart—105 rounds compared to 70.

An 1870s picture of a French soldier with a Chassepot rifle
Source: *https://commons.wikimedia.org/wiki/File:Soldier-chassepot.jpg*

An 1870 illustration of a mitrailleuse crew
Source: https://commons.wikimedia.org/wiki/File:Mitrailleuse_bollee.jpg

Besides the standard issue rifle, the French also developed the Montigny-Reffye mitrailleuse, named after the grapeshot, or *mitraille* in French. It was originally developed by the Belgian engineer Joseph Montigny during the 1850s, before Napoleon III expressed an interest in its concept. Montigny worked with Jean-Baptiste Verchère de Reffye to create the mitrailleuse in 1865. It was an early type of a machine gun, similar to the contemporary Gatling gun, with a number of rifle barrels strapped to an artillery chassis. The original Montigny design used thirty-seven barrels, while the later Montigny-Reffye had twenty-five barrels. The mitrailleuse used a hand-cranked mechanism to transform it into a rapid-firing gun. The cranking mechanism gave it the nickname *moulin à café*, or "coffee grinder." It was breech loaded with cartridges, thus making the overall rate of fire dependent on the skill of the four-man crew operating it. Nevertheless, with an average of one hundred to two hundred rounds per minute, it outgunned any conventional rifle. It also had an effective range of around 1,200 yards (1,100 meters), going up to a maximum of at least 2,000 yards (1,830 meters). During testing, a stray bullet reportedly managed to kill a villager about 3,000 yards (2,740 meters) away. Furthermore, its 13-

millimeter (0.512-inch) ammo was packed with twice the amount of gunpowder used by the Chassepot, giving it high muzzle velocity and stopping power.

This novel weapon was initially kept a secret, but eventually, its existence was witnessed by the Prussians. Nonetheless, the German forces didn't have anything comparable in their arsenal, nor were there any signs of attempting to develop a similar rapid-firing gun. Despite seeing its devastating potential, Prussian observers noted that it showed notable vulnerability, as it lacked any shield or cover, making its crew exposed to enemy fire. Its range meant it had to be relatively in the front lines as well, unlike proper artillery. Regardless, both the Chassepot and the mitrailleuse swayed the firepower balance toward the French side, at least on paper. The only armament in which the Prussian had the upper hand was artillery.

The French were using the so-called La Hitte cannons, a muzzle-loaded bored gun that fired shells weighing 4 kilograms (8.8 pounds). It was designed in 1858 and introduced the following year, proving to be a powerful novelty in the war against the Austrians. At the time, bored barrels were a newly implemented technology, allowing the gun to fire heavier projectiles farther. Its maximum range was reported at about 3,280 yards (3,000 meters). However, the French shells used timed fuses, which had only two settings, exploding either at 1,200 yards (1,100 meters) or at 2,500 yards (2,285 meters), making its "kill zones" rather limited, at least when it came to explosive rounds. Regardless, the French seemed satisfied with their artillery and were convinced that it was still competitive on the 1870 battlefield. In contrast, the Prussians faced similar technology against the Austrians in 1866 and realized their old smoothbore cannons were inadequate. Thus, they invested in developing new artillery technology, producing the cutting-edge Krupp six-pounder.

This gun was introduced in between two Prussian wars, and it adopted not only bored barrels but also breechloading technology. Additionally, the cannon itself was made out of steel instead of the bronze used by the French for their guns. All of that made the Krupp fire more accurately, have at least a third longer range, and have a rate of fire that was twice as fast. Further improvements were made in the realm of the shell itself. Despite its name, the weight of Krupp's projectiles was actually 6 kilograms or 13.2 pounds. That, of course, meant a higher destructive power. Finally, the shells were fitted with percussion detonated fuses, making their operational ranges much wider than of the French La Hitte. Both the Krupp and the Chassepot paint a picture of both sides preparing for war and improving upon what they deemed were their weakest points in terms of armament technology. However, artillery deficiency was a substantial French blunder, as the Krupp Works, an independent German steel and arms producer from Essen, offered its six-pounder to them as well. Yet, their high command lacked the foresight to accept and implement this clearly superior weapon. Because of that, in terms of firepower, the French Army held only a slight superiority.

However, the supposed troops or weapons superiority on paper was one thing. It is a totally different question of how the two commands used them. Like with most aspects of the military so far mentioned, the tactics used by the French and the Prussians differed greatly. The first jarring contrast laid on the grand strategic scheme. Despite the French being the ones to officially declare the war, their overall plans rested on a defensive footing. The basic idea was to identify important positions where the French troops would best stop a German invasion. There were some ideas about crossing the Rhine and forcing the southern Germanic states from the war, but most of the French high command feared such a move would leave the road to Paris open to invaders. The only hope for that kind of flanking assault laid in Austria and Italy entering the war, as there could be a tripartite strike in the Prussian underbelly. On the other hand, the Prussians planned an offensive war. The basic idea put down by Moltke was to strike fast and in a flanking manner, not only disrupting the French defensive lines but also their lines of communications and supplies.

The tactical differences didn't end there. The French, like in many other military aspects, remained more conservative and traditional. Their infantry was grouped in battalions, which were tightly grouped to utilize their superior rifle, and the men fired in an organized fashion. It was a perfect tactic for disrupting enemy advances. Furthermore, the French soldiers were trained in digging trenches and defenses. This rather defensive positioning was further strengthened by artillery, which was formed in the so-called "great batteries" behind the infantry. Such highly concentrated firepower would be able to pulverize any massive attack coming their way. Finally, behind all of those rather tightly packed lines was the cavalry. The French put an emphasis on heavy cavalry, which was tasked with making decisive blows and breakthroughs, and gave little attention to light cavalry, whose roles were usually more toward reconnaissance. It was a staggering grip upon tradition, ignoring the fact that the evolution of firearms made any straightforward cavalry charge pretty much suicide. Events in the Crimean War, most notably the infamous British charge of the light brigade at Balaclava, as well as the Battle of Königgrätz (1866), showcased that to any sensible observer.

An 1875 painting of French cavalry from the Franco-Prussian War capturing Bavarian infantry.
Source: https://commons.wikimedia.org/wiki/File:Detaille_-
A French Cavalry Officer Guarding Captured Bavarian Soldiers.jpg

Yet, when the entirety of the French tactics is summed up, they were aimed at creating a static, tightly packed defensive line, with the intention of utilizing both the Chassepot and the mitrailleuse to overwhelm advancing forces. The cavalry was supposed to chase the enemy away once they were already stunned. On paper, such an approach made sense, but only if the enemy employed the traditional attacking strategy of rolling toward them in a massive line. What the French commanders, for the most part, failed to acknowledge was the fact that the Prussians adopted new tactics in all aspects of warfare, making their defensive lines largely obsolete. Even worse, when they did notice the changes, they thought of them as a flaw, not an improvement. Such thinking was voiced clearly in their judgment of Prussian infantry tactics.

Unlike the French, Moltke's basic thought was maneuverability and flexibility on the battlefield. To achieve that, he gave the company the capability of breaking down into even smaller platoons. The French commanders thought these smaller units would be more easily gunned down, especially with their superior rifles. However, they disregarded the fact that Moltke never intended to send his troops straight at their lines. The Prussians would spread, flank, and encircle the fixed positions of their enemies. In this way, they would be only small targets while attacking from all sides, making concentrated fire almost impossible. To make such maneuvers as smooth as possible, soldiers not only practiced how to transition from marching order into attacking order but also how to form improvised companies from mismatched platoons when necessary, further speeding things up. Furthermore, they decentralized their command to a degree while maintaining the coherency of their battle plan by issuing large-scale maps to their lower-ranking officers, allowing them to find their way on unfamiliar terrain.

Nevertheless, the superior range of the Chassepot and the firepower of the mitrailleuse were still an issue for the Prussian infantry. To mitigate that, Moltke reformed his artillery as well. Instead of going for passive and static "great batteries," he created so-called "artillery masses." Those were smaller and more mobile artillery batteries that could move and redeploy across the battlefield where needed. With that, they could be massed in one spot or dispersed in several positions, possibly firing from several different angles. On top of that, they often went much closer to the infantry than any other contemporary army, allowing for shorter ranges and increased accuracy of fire. To combat the risk of leaving certain points of their own lines without crucial artillery cover, the artillery batteries were issued orders to work toward the same ultimate goal as the infantry. Overall, such tactics added another layer to Prussian mobility while negating the superiority of the French rifles.

Moltke also painstakingly worked on transforming the Prussian cavalry, which he himself saw as the worst part of his army. Realizing that the time of frontal cavalry charges was over, he reformed the calvary into smaller and lighter units. Its main role became supporting the infantry, not working as an independent section of an army.

Unlike the French, the Prussian cavalry primarily went on reconnaissance and escort missions while also often acting as the front and rearguard. Furthermore, as they were divided into smaller units, they were deployed all over the battlefield. Their roles presented the pinnacle of the new Prussian tactics of maneuverability and flexibility. One Prussian officer described them as an elastic band, encircling the enemy and retreating when he advances but following him when he retreats. The Prussian cavalry also exhibited decentralization. Not only did they divide into squadrons but also into squads and even down to a single scouting rider.

These overall divisions and subdivisions of the Prussian Army, with smaller regiments acting individually to a degree, seemed like anarchy to many foreign observers. Yet, in reality, it represented a fine-tuned military machine, compromised of numerous smaller moving parts working toward a single goal. This was achieved through the idea of the so-called "mission tactics," or *Auftragstaktik*. In essence, this meant that officers had freedom of judgment over how to carry out their orders as long as they were still following the intent and plan of the high command. Such bureaucratic leadership greatly increased the efficiency of the Prussian military without creating a mess in their own lines. It also meant that lower-ranked officers could exploit favorable positions while preventing disasters by mending their own tactical disadvantages without waiting for confirmation from the *Generalstab*.

Finally, it is significant to mention that the Prussian military was the first in Europe to utilize modern civilian technologies to its own benefit, most notably railways and the telegraph. Realizing the potential of trains for carrying supplies and troops, the Prussian military diverted its infrastructural spending from fortresses to railways, both private- and state-owned. This created a functional railway network in militarily useful regions, giving them the infrastructure needed for massive troop movements. That sped up both mobilization and deployment of units while easing their resupplying and reinforcements. The French, on the other hand, had substantial issues with their underdeveloped railways, which were almost exclusively in private hands. Any substantial military use required a lot of bureaucratic work to be done. As for the telegraph, Moltke was the first general to fully rely on these electronic messages to relay his orders. This not only sped up the transfer of information and reactions from the General Staff but also allowed simultaneous coordination of much more complicated maneuvers and tactics.

Overall, it is clear that, in most cases, the French and the Prussian forces were almost polar opposites. One side stuck to time-tested traditional military doctrines, while the other went on to innovate and ultimately transform how armies functioned. In hindsight, it is clear whose approach was better, but it is vital to remember that, at the time, not many were so sure, apart from maybe Moltke and his inner circle.

Chapter 4 – The Battle Begins: Initial Positioning and Opening Clashes

Despite both nations being on the verge of war for years, neither was actually immediately prepared for a conflict. Both needed some time to mobilize their troops, as well as time to arm and deploy them. Thus, the principal concern in the early days of the Franco-Prussian War was the speed of mobilization and positioning of soldiers.

For the French, this was a "make or break moment," as they held the early edge. They had a larger active army, and according to the high command, it could be deployed to the border in a fortnight. On the other hand, they expected that the Prussians needed at least seven weeks to mobilize their forces to gain superiority in numbers. There laid a possibility for France to strike first, hopefully enticing Austria, Denmark, and Italy to join in while simultaneously derailing Prussian mobilization. Such an offensive action was expected by the French public, which yearned to "punish" the Prussians for their insolence. However, the French command didn't actually have any fully fleshed out plans. Instead, Napoleon III tried to accommodate both offensive and defensive actions. He split his army into three pieces: I Corps under Marshal Patrice MacMahon in Alsace, VI Corps under Marshal François Canrobert at Châlons, and the Army of the Rhine under his imperial command at Metz. Though named "corps," the first two groupings were actually army-sized.

The naming of those provides a glimpse into the issues plaguing the French high command. The emperor wanted to capitalize on a possible military victory for himself, making his army groupings reminiscent of his uncle's more famous *Grande Armée*. Thus, in a sense, he exiled his most celebrated and capable marshals to field the "smaller" corps, while one of his best commanders, if not his best commander, Marshal Achille Bazaine, was only given provisional command over his army in Metz until Napoleon arrived from Paris. However, Bazaine was under strict orders not to do anything without his permission. Adding insult to injury, members of his imperial headquarters consisted of the freshly promoted Marshal Edmond Leboeuf and Generals Lebrun and Jarras. Together with Napoleon himself, the headquarters had almost no actual military experience. After arriving at Metz on July 28th, the emperor tried to ask Bazaine for assistance in planning an offensive, yet the marshal had no advice to offer. On the other hand, MacMahon tried to show some initiative, asking for some orders on how to proceed in the case of a French assault, but he was ignored. In the end, Leboeuf and Lebrun chose a defensive course of action, massing the Army of the Rhine in Lorraine and waiting for the Prussians.

However, the cracks in the leadership were only the tip of Napoleon's troubles. By late July, only about two-thirds of the planned forces were deployed on the front line. The railways were congested, and troops arrived in smaller, often disjointed groups, commonly without their primary armaments. This meant that units needed to be assembled and armed after arriving, which led to some soldiers not being battle-ready upon arrival at the border. Furthermore, eagerness for the war quickly dissipated, both among the troops and common citizens. This forced Napoleon to leave about fifteen thousand valuable troops in Paris to secure his reign while he was on the front. Realizing that the regular 400,000 to 500,000 troops the high command counted on most likely wouldn't be enough, a call for volunteers was issued. In a nation with a population of about thirty-five million, only four thousand enlisted, showing how little the French actually cared for the war by then. All the while, soldier morale and discipline were at a horrendous low point. Many were dropping parts of their equipment, while whole units would just wander off to a nearby village or town, looking for some entertainment. Common recruits simply ignored their officers whenever they felt like it.

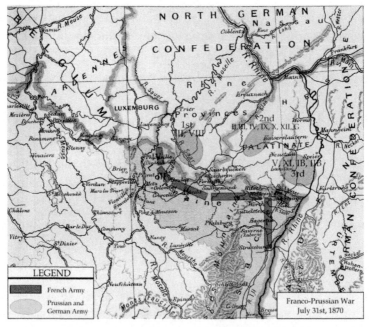

A map depicting the initial positions of both the French and the Prussian forces.
Source: https://commons.wikimedia.org/wiki/File:FrancoPrussianWarFrontierJuly1870.jpg

Moreover, they often questioned their orders and instructions, which went all the way up to the emperor himself. They doubted even the larger strategic picture, despite often having no grasp of the tactics. Overall, this proved to be a personal blow to Napoleon, whose regime was supposed to be a military one, one that was secured by a loyal army. France's position in the war seemed to worsen by the day, despite the projections for an early advantage. In contrast, the Germans only gained strength as mobilization went on.

Initially, the proclamation of war caught Moltke and his General Staff off guard. Many Prussian officers were given leave just a few days prior; thus, he had to scramble to recall them all. Nevertheless, the Prussian military practiced mobilization during peacetime, and it quickly started rolling out. Officers planned railway routes and the transportation of their units, sending them to designated grouping areas. Thanks to their much better railroad system, Prussians had about five times as many trains running daily compared to the French. All of that made Prussian mobilization an organized event rather than the ad hoc mess of their opponents, even though it wasn't a fully expected war. It is interesting to mention that another organizational improvement the Prussian military made just prior to the war was the introduction of modern metal dog tags; it was the first modern army in the world to do so. Though this improvement did little to help functionality and mobilization, as it served only as an identification tool for fallen soldiers, it does showcase how well prepared the Prussian Army had become.

In the years prior to the war, Moltke toured down the front lines, inspecting the expected concentration areas and ironing out any inefficiencies and liabilities. He was aware that mobilization was never a simple affair, no matter how well thought out it was. This was especially true for the Prussians' south Germanic allies. There were some accounts of their trains being overcrowded, units getting sunburnt during their marches toward the front, and drunken disobedience, caused by soldiers drinking alcohol instead of water. It is likely similar pictures could've been seen among the Prussian troops but to a much lesser extent. Regardless, the overall German discipline was much higher than among the French.

The Prussian home front was also in much better spirits than the French, with many enlisting on their own. According to some contemporaries, almost all able-bodied men between twenty and thirty-eight years of age were conscripted. Although this is clearly an exaggeration, it paints a picture of Prussian morale and the functionality of its military conscription system. However, a substantial number of volunteers were young university students whose fitness and training were subpar. They simply didn't have enough time to prepare under the Prussian service system. Nevertheless, they compensated for those failings with their enthusiasm. Combining that general fighting spirit with a well-organized mobilization system allowed the Prussian forces to gather 320,000 battle-ready troops by the early days of August. They caught up with French numerical superiority much quicker than most expected.

While the troops amassed, Moltke initially positioned his troops behind the Rhine, Saar, and Moselle Rivers, using them as a natural barrier if the French attacked first. While they amassed, he divided his forces into three armies. The First Army was under the command of General Karl von Steinmetz, and it was located in the northernmost sector of the front line, between Trier and Saarlouis. In the center was the Second Army, commanded by the king's nephew, Prince Friedrich Karl. It was located near Saarbrücken, and it represented the largest of the Prussian forces. Crown Prince Friedrich Wilhelm, the heir to the Prussian throne, was given control of the Third Army, which was positioned around Karlsruhe in the south. As it was to be expected, this southernmost force mostly consisted of the southern Germanic allies—Bavaria, Baden, and Württemberg. Moltke remained skeptical about them joining in the war until the very end and thus refused to supply their junior officers with the same detailed maps Prussians used. It is also worth noting that these troops were caught in the middle of rearming with the newer breechloading rifle.

Finally, unlike Napoleon and his indecisive staff, Moltke and the *Generalstab* were more than prepared to utilize their troops to the best of their extent. In case the French concentrated their troops in the south, either defensively or to attack Baden, the First and Second Armies would push into France, swinging to the southwest to flank. In contrast, if Napoleon decided to keep his troops at Metz or even try to invade the Rhineland, the Third Army would maneuver into the French rear, cutting off communications with Paris and flanking the Army of the Rhine. During the last days of July, the French Army began preparations to do exactly that. Napoleon and his command began to feel public pressure to do something, and even General Charles Frossard, one of his favorite officers, had advocated for days that they attack the border town of Saarbrücken. On July 29th, 1870, the emperor authorized the attack, and the French soldiers began positioning for an advance into Germany.

However, this attack proved to be more of a publicity stunt for the emperor. His troops attacked on August 2nd, encountering only sporadic resistance by the Prussians, mostly skirmishing with their patrols. In those small-scale conflicts, their Chassepot proved its superiority, for the German forces usually scattered. As the French divisions approached Saarbrücken, the single Prussian division defending it more or less withdrew, so no major combat took place. Upon taking hold of the town, Napoleon and Frossard immediately hailed it as a grand victory, something even the belligerent French public had a hard time believing. Such pompousness was quickly debunked since the French Army withdrew almost as quickly as it invaded after realizing that the Prussians were finalizing their initial mobilization and moving their troops across the Rhine toward them.

Overall, the brief invasion of Saarbrücken was not only an exercise in futility but also a serious blunder. Firstly, it further deteriorated the relations between Marshal Bazaine and Napoleon III. Bazaine, who had more experience and a higher rank than Frossard, was relegated to a supporting position. Bazaine himself knew that there was no point to this attack unless the French Army was to push hard and deep into Prussia, which was unreal. Despite that, he tried to organize a proper enveloping advance onto Saarbrücken, but he was plainly ignored. From then on, Marshal Bazaine became more obstructive than cooperative. Even worse was the fact that this half-measured attack proved that the emperor had no military talent, ordering troops that were a linking pin between the Army of the Rhine and MacMahon's I Corps farther south to join in the attack on Saarbrücken. Without thinking it through, Napoleon and Leboeuf basically left MacMahon without the proper support he would dearly need in the upcoming days.

Marshal Bazaine
Source: https://commons.wikimedia.org/wiki/File:Bazaine_Disd%C3%A9ri_BNF_Gallica.jpg

Marshal MacMahon
Source: https://commons.wikimedia.org/wiki/File:Patrice_de_Mac-Mahon.jpg

Such a miscalculation could also be partially attributed to French intelligence. While the Prussian cavalry constantly roamed the border regions, French reconnaissance was sporadic and shoddy. Most information coming to Napoleon and his headquarters came from newspapers and foreign war correspondents, which were aided by their own conjectures. When the French ordered the attack on Saarbrücken, it's likely they had little clue that the Prussians were only a few days away from being ready for an invasion of their own. Seeing that the French were basically holding their lines at Metz, disregarding the tactically irrelevant advance on Saarbrücken, Moltke decided to swing the Third Army into MacMahon's I Corps, driving into the Vosges mountain range, before swinging to the north and forcing the French into a pocket. It was a calculated risk on his part, as it would essentially cut off Crown Prince Friedrich Wilhelm's Third Army from the rest of the Prussian forces for several days. Yet, Moltke had all the confidence in the crown prince and his numerical superiority of 125,000 Germans against MacMahon's 45,000 French soldiers.

The French high command, for the most part, was unaware of exact German movements but got wind of it from captured Prussian soldiers and a local chief of police who noticed the enemy approaching. It was these scraps of intelligence that forced the French to retreat from Saarbrücken to their original defensive positions by August 5th, yet by then, MacMahon's corps was under attack. The Prussian Third Army made its initial engagement a day before, attacking a single French division defending Wissembourg. It was an 18th-century defensive fort that overlooked an important junction for Bavaria, Strasbourg, and Lower Alsace. However, in the years prior to the war, that fortification lost its funding, and its state was far from ideal. Further adding to MacMahon's trouble was the fact that he had only four divisions in total, spread to cover the entire southern French flank across the Vosges, making his lines too thinly spread. This meant that it was unlikely he had enough time to react and reposition his men in the case of a Prussian advance.

By the early morning of August 4th, the French cavalry finally made contact with the advancing German troops. A local official had noticed the German movements and alarmed the local French authorities the day before. However, it was dismissed as an insignificant border clash. While the Wissembourg command was reporting it as such, the Prussian artillery began its bombardment. Initially, the French seemed to have an advantage. Using their fortified positions and superior firepower of the Chassepot and the mitrailleuse, they pummeled the Bavarian soldiers who crossed the Lauter River that ran in front of the fort. The mitrailleuse filled the attacking soldiers with special dread, as it often tore bodies into shreds. The French artillery also managed to have an initial impact, showering the advancing troops with their shells. Nonetheless, the French quickly lost their advantage. The Prussian command was aware they had only a single division, one that was tightly packed in the town and its fortification. This made their usual enveloping tactics work almost perfectly as they began spreading out, surrounding the defensive forces. Soon, a few of the Prussian artillery guns also crossed the river, providing a more accurate supportive fire and limiting how effectively the French garrison could fire at the advancing forces.

As the town itself became engulfed in door-to-door combat, its inhabitants, led by their mayor, began pleading with the French soldiers to retreat and to spare their homes from what they saw as a futile resistance. Parts of the French troops were routed, an act likely facilitated by the fact that their commanding officer was killed early in the day from artillery bombardment shrapnel. Other French troops, especially those that were encircled in the town, had no other option than to fight. They chose to make a stoic stand. However, in the end, they were overrun, and by the afternoon, Wissembourg was in German hands. Despite that, the casualties were similar on both sides, with about 1,500 men killed and wounded, though several hundred more Frenchmen were captured.

An illustration from 1899 depicting the close combat at Wissembourg.

After the battle, the Prussian commanders realized two important things. One was that the French tactic of grouping their entire divisions in an effort to maximize their firepower was wrong, though intuitive. The Chassepot was indeed a much better rifle, both in precision and range, but by condensing their soldiers in one spot, the French were just making it easier for the Prussians to pummel them with their superior artillery, breaking both their spirits and defenses while flanking them surprisingly easy. The second lesson was that their Bavarian allies were only slightly better soldiers than the French. They lacked discipline, especially when under fire. Without the training the Prussians went through, their allies fired too quickly and without proper aim, ignoring direct orders and looking for any reason to break the fire line. Furthermore, after the battle was done, the Bavarians led the looting, searching for food and drink. The Prussians' discipline would be hammered into them in the following weeks.

As the German Third Army was advancing in the south, Moltke began to orchestrate his overarching plan of forcing the French Army into a cauldron. He planned to strike at the heart of Napoleon's forces with the strong Second Army, with the principal target being Frossard's new positions at Spicheren and Forbach, an important supply depot for the French. By attacking at the center and aiming at such an important target, Moltke hoped to suck in the rest of the French troops while the First Army moved up from the north and the Third Army from the south. It was a reasonable plan, despite the fact that the Third Army still hadn't moved through the Vosges yet. However, Moltke's grand design was almost ruined by General Steinmetz. Despite being a grizzled veteran, in 1870, he was far past his prime. Some of his peers even claimed he was slipping into senility. Nevertheless, he was the people's hero and a close friend to King Wilhelm, assuring his commanding position. Having such a strong position in the Prussian Army, Steinmetz decided to take matters into his own hands and ignored Moltke's orders. Instead of taking his forces, the smallest of the three German armies, across the

Saar River on the Second Army's right flank to feel out the French positions there, he swiped south toward Frossard.

This proved to be a critical error. With such an irrational movement, Steinmetz cut off the advance of the Second Army under Prince Friedrich Karl, who methodically followed Moltke's plan. Thus, it was the First Army that engaged the center of the French forces, though not on Steinmetz's direct orders. One of his divisional generals reached Spicheren on August 6th and thought the French were retreating. Thus, he ordered a full-on attack on what was supposed to be the French rearguard. Yet, in reality, General Frossard dug in the superior positions around it, using the hilly terrain to his advantage, and he had no plans to yield. Moltke's plan was on the brink of destruction at that moment, as the French held far superior positions while the Prussian attack was made without any regard to grand strategic development. And all because of the overzealousness of Steinmetz and his subordinate officer.

Beyond the initial miscalculation of the French forces, Steinmetz's division general made another mistake. He attacked without having all his troops with him, sending just a couple of battalions, which arrived first. When initial contact was made, the strength of French fire signaled that it wasn't merely a rearguard. The Prussian forces came close to the French positions but were stopped in their tracks by the French guns. For a while, the German artillery was able to keep the French forces at bay, but by the afternoon, the Prussian troops took too many casualties and began retreating. Frossard then allowed for a formidable counterattack, which managed to push back both the retreating German forces as well as the troops that were just arriving on the battlefield. Had he unleashed the full potential of the French forces, he might have dealt a painful defeat to the Prussians. Yet, he clung to the defensive strategy, refusing to leave the safety of his fortified high ground. That gave enough time for the Prussians to regroup.

Soon, Prince Friedrich Karl's units began to arrive, immediately shifting to fighting formations without waiting for the direct command to do so. More importantly, Steinmetz's division general was relieved of command, giving the reins to the more competent General Constantin von Alvensleben. The Prussians then began to amass their troops and once again increased pressure on the French, slowly pushing them back while simultaneously fanning out to begin proper encirclement. Frossard's men continued to rain shells on the attackers, but here, the proper Prussian discipline, stubbornness, and numerical superiority began to shine through. They continued to advance relentlessly, maintaining their skirmish lines despite casualties. All the while, the Prussian artillery not only grew in size but also found more favorable positions, increasing their pressure on the French defenses. By the late afternoon, Alvensleben had gathered enough of his own troops as reserves to thrust them at the French flanks. Combined with artillery fire, this proved enough to dislodge the French from Spicheren. By the evening, Frossard ordered a full retreat back to the defensive line on the Moselle River.

An 1890 drawing of Prussian troops advancing at Spicheren.
Source: *https://commons.wikimedia.org/wiki/File:Spicheren-Roter_Berg.png*

Thus, Spicheren was nearly a disaster for the Prussians. It was avoided more by French blunders than anything else. Had Frossard unleashed a proper counterattack, the Germans would have most likely shattered. Furthermore, the battle lasted long enough for him to receive reinforcements, but the faulty relations and communication between French commanders led to disaster. Frossard initially asked for just two brigades, but Bazaine refused to send them. His lines were already thin, he said, while at the time, Frossard was still unsure if the Prussian attack was a serious one. The animosity between the two officers only dulled Bazaine's willingness to aid his compatriot. However, had Frossard asked properly and timely for reinforcements, Bazaine surely wouldn't have let him down. Yet, in the early afternoon, Frossard messaged him, saying that he believed he would be victorious, mistaking the Prussian respite for defeat. Only a couple of hours later, he sent a telegram stating he had been outflanked and on the verge of defeat. By then, it was too late, as Bazaine's troops needed several hours to arrive. In fact, Bazaine sent a full division to Frossard, but they managed to arrive only as his soldiers were retreating.

In the end, the Battle of Spicheren exemplified significant characteristics on both sides. For better or worse, the Prussian officers showed more proactivity and acted upon their own instincts, while the French were reined in by their orders. The latter were also constricted by their overly defensive strategy, while the Prussians showed their tenacity and stubbornness to push through the mud and grit. It also showcased the swarming feature of the Prussian advance. They often made contact with the French with a limited number of troops, testing out their defenses while slowly amassing their troops for an attack if the opportunity seemed right. This made it rather hard for the French commanders to determine if the clash was a mere skirmish or a full-blown attack. By the time they figured it out, it usually proved too late. Spicheren also showed how deadly the battles could be, as both sides suffered substantial losses. The Prussians casualties were just below five thousand out of a force of about thirty-seven thousand, while the

French were around four thousand of a total twenty-nine thousand soldiers. Nevertheless, these were merely initial clashes and were still limited in scope.

Chapter 5 – Spreading the Flames of War: The Prussian Invasion

The victories of Wissembourg and Spicheren were only the opening scenes in what was soon to become a French tragedy. As the German First and Second Armies were only springing into action, the Third Army, under Crown Prince Friedrich Wilhelm, began to push deeper into French territory.

He planned to deal with MacMahon on the eastern slopes of the Vosges, securing his rear, before swiveling north to aid the main Prussian attack. After Wissembourg, his troops lost contact with the retreating French troops; thus, on August 5th, the German cavalry spread around the region, searching for the enemy. Friedrich Wilhelm thought MacMahon retreated to the safety of the fortress in Strasbourg, farther to the south. Instead, his scouts found the French I Corps entrenched at Froeschwiller-Woerth, a group of villages in the Vosges only twelve miles (twenty kilometers) southeast of Wissembourg. Such a decision was backed both strategically and tactically. Firstly, Froeschwiller was an important railroad junction. If the Prussians seized it, it would isolate the forces in Strasbourg while easing German resupplying. In tactical terms, it was one of *positions magnifique*, as the French called them, a location that was easily defendable. The four villages compromising the Froeschwiller-Woerth basin were linked by a lateral road, so it was easily enforceable. They held the high ground while also forming a semicircular line with the Sauer River beneath them. Most positions had clear fields of fire in all directions, while the hill slopes were dotted with vine and hop plantations, making advancing through them a nightmare for the attackers. Indeed, the Froeschwiller-Woerth was a position that could make the most out of the Chassepot and the mitrailleuse.

Nevertheless, the Froeschwiller-Woerth basin had one major defensive flaw. It was exposed to flanking and encirclement, especially if no other troops were near enough to support its defense. All that the Prussians needed to achieve a victory was sufficient numerical superiority, which they had. The Third Army that marched toward Froeschwiller-Woerth numbered almost 100,000 men, while there were only 50,000 French defenders. Despite that, MacMahon still planned his counterattack. In the early hours of August 6th, he ordered the nearby V Corps, which was thirty thousand men strong under General Pierre de Failly, to be prepared for either attacking the Prussian flank as they moved through the Vosges or even encirclement if the enemy proved inactive. Regardless of MacMahon's wishful thinking, Crown Prince Friedrich Wilhelm was diligent and planned to use his numerical advantage to flank and surround the French forces. Furthermore, he planned to do it properly, gathering his army and attacking the fortified positions in an organized manner. Yet, like at Spicheren, one of the middle-ranked officers hotheadedly committed to an early attack.

As forward units of several Third Army corps unexpectedly stumbled upon the French positions, their commanding officer ordered his men to attack immediately, without waiting for the rest of the Third Army. Thus, the Battle of Froeschwiller-Woerth began on

August 6th instead of on August 7th as the crown prince had planned. To make matters worse, they faced the French left wing, which was held by numerous battle-hardened veterans who served in Crimea, Algeria, and Italy. As the gunfire began to echo, the arriving Prussian troops immediately began deploying into battle lines, expanding the existing German front line. Friedrich Wilhelm was furious and tried to delay the battle, sending messengers to the forward lines, but it was too late. Froeschwiller-Woerth was turning into an another Spicheren.

The initial clashes at Froeschwiller-Woerth were eerily similar to the battle that raged at roughly the same time near Spicheren. The first attacks, carried out by mixed Prussian, Bavarian, and Baden-Württembergian troops, thinned their advancing columns into skirmish lines, slowly enfolding the French positions. Yet, their advance was almost nonexistent, as the defenders picked them off with their superior rifles and the mitrailleuse, which were further supported by their artillery. The marshy and hilly battleground only further bogged down the German advance, while the surrounding woods provided little cover against the French cannons. Even the best trained Prussian soldiers stood little chance as the defenders rained down upon them with hot lead. The German casualties piled up, and some of the troops even lost their nerve and ran away from combat, most notably the Bavarians. As the day approached noon, the battle was slipping away from the Germans, and if the French had mounted a timely counterattack, the Germans could have faltered. Yet, once again, the French command decided to remain on the defense.

Trying to salvage the battle, Friedrich Wilhelm sent two of his adjutants to rein in and organize the assault, as the crown prince was literally stuck in traffic traveling to Froeschwiller-Woerth. Upon their arrival, his adjutants found some friction between the Prussians and the Bavarians. The latter felt they were being sacrificed to save Prussian lives, despite all of them dying along the front line. Some of the Bavarian officers even refused to commit their troops to an attack, agreeing to do so only under direct pressure from the crown prince.

Nevertheless, the Third Army corps continued to roll in, expanding their flanks and slowly encircling MacMahon. More importantly, the German artillery began arriving in greater numbers and started pummeling French defensive positions. As the battle dragged on, the artillery fire began to suppress the defenders, simultaneously countering the French cannons, destroying their mitrailleuse nests, and demoralizing the troops. The significance of the Prussian artillery is illustrated by the French commanders who claimed that without it, they would have easily defended against any German assault.

A battle position at Froeschwiller-Woerth depicting Prussian cauldron tactics
Source:
https://commons.wikimedia.org/wiki/File:Karte_zur_Schlacht_bei_W%C3%B6rth_(06.08.18 70).jpg

Prussian artillery moving through the streets of Woerth
Source: https://commons.wikimedia.org/wiki/File:Batteries_passed_through_the_streets.jpg

By the early afternoon, the Third Army was deployed almost in its full strength. The envelopment was finalizing, leaving MacMahon with a single option to restore his battle fortunes. He ordered his heavy cavalry reserves to charge at the advancing Prussian flanks; in other words, it was a last resort, "Hail Mary" attempt. The counterattack quickly turned into a disaster, as the Prussian rapid-firing guns proved the era of cavalry charges was gone. None of the French horsemen managed to get near the German lines. With that, the battle was pretty much resolved. The Prussians' relentless advance and artillery fire began to wear down the French, especially on their right flank, which lacked experience, being compromised mostly of freshly recruited troops. They crumbled and fled, leaving flanks and the rear of the rest of MacMahon's corps exposed, which the German troops immediately used to their advantage. Additionally, the Prussian troops and artillery harassed the retreating French troops. Soon, the French left wing began to falter, while the German troops managed to advance even on the heavily defended center. One by one, the French divisions fell into disarray, retreating in mass panic. There were some valiant exceptions among the French, but they were easily silenced by the swarming Prussian troops. By late afternoon, it was clear the battle was won by the Third Army.

As night fell, darkness covered up the scattering of what remained of MacMahon's I Corps, preventing even more devastating results. The end tally for the French was about twenty thousand; about half were wounded and killed, while the rest were captured. It represents a loss of about 40 percent of the I Corps. On the German side, the losses were around ten thousand, or just 10 percent of the Third Army's strength. With losses in men as well as in equipment, the French I Corps was knocked out of the war for a while, allowing the crown prince to choose if he wanted to pursue them or close on the Army of the Rhine at Metz. With the victory at Froeschwiller-Woerth, the Germans showed the French and the rest of the world that their invasion, unlike the initial French theatrics near Saarbrücken, was a serious undertaking.

It should be noted that at Froeschwiller-Woerth, apart from their loose and opportunistic tactics, the Germans exhibited their less-than-civilized face. Despite this war being a struggle between two nations, the two armies also had some non-national troops. On the Prussian side, those were Poles, while the French had their Algerian Berber troops. At one point during the battle, the latter were exhibiting stiff resistance, despite being surrounded. The Algerian regiment fought on, causing frustration to the attackers. The Prussians and Bavarians began claiming that the Berbers were committing various atrocities, mutilating and killing the wounded Germans, despite not really being in a position to do so. Thus, they began their revenge, hunting them down and executing every wounded Algerian they found. Such monstrous behavior was only eased by the fact that the Berbers were seen as beast-like dark-skinned barbarians. Even Bismarck later approved of such actions, claiming that Algerians, or as he called them "black men," "are beasts of prey, and ought to be shot down."

Regardless of such vile outbursts, the Germans continued their advance through France. For days, they were met without any serious opposition as their troops plundered and looted the French countryside, looking for supplies they needed. As they slowly enclosed around the main body of the French Army, France was slowly dissolving into internal turmoil. In Paris, the military violently suppressed outbursts of disappointment when Ollivier was replaced. The new prime minister was General Charles Cousin de Montauban, who was much more on the extreme right side of the political spectrum and a person much closer to Napoleon III. Regardless, Paris was slowly descending into a revolutionary atmosphere similar to 1789 and 1848. The emperor was losing public support, while defeatism began to corrode the French masses, though their national zeal kept some of the fighting spirit alive.

The losses at Spicheren and Froeschwiller-Woerth caused ripples in the French military organization and hierarchy as well. Napoleon reluctantly and gradually relinquished control over the Army of the Rhine to Marshal Bazaine. It was only on August 11th, when the legislative body in Paris tried to impeach Leboeuf, that the emperor realized he had to hand over command to Bazaine regardless of their personal rivalries. Yet, Napoleon still dragged this on as long as he could, even forcing Bazaine to take in members of Leboeuf's cabinet into his staff. It was only on August 14th that Bazaine finally was given full control of the main body of the French Army, although the emperor still tried to influence the marshal's decisions, playing on his official title of commander-in-chief. As Napoleon and Bazaine were playing this tug-of-war, the French troops stood still, doing nothing and losing vital time for any maneuvers. They remained centered around Metz. All the while, Moltke's three armies were gradually enveloping them. By August 14th, his cavalry units were already biting into the communication lines between Metz and Paris.

It is only around this time that the first French units began moving away from Metz; however, this was both too late and too leisurely.

The main problem facing the French defenders was the fact that Metz lay on the eastern banks of the Moselle River, which was open to Prussian attacks. On August 13th, Napoleon issued Bazaine an order to retreat westward to Verdun, falling as far back as Châlons. He refused, claiming that retreating at that moment was unfavorable since the Germans were arriving. By that time, the Third Army was closing in from the south, taking control of Nancy, a junction in the principal supply line for the Prussians. More surprisingly, the French allowed that without a fight. By doing so, Bazaine's only line of retreat was, in fact, via Verdun. Yet, by August 14th, the German First Army clashed with Bazaine's rearguard of the Army of the Rhine. A short and rather half-hearted battle took place at Borny, on the outskirts of Metz.

This conflict was instigated by middle-ranked Prussian officers, but this time, Steinmetz reined in his troops. He didn't want to commit to the attack, fearing more reprimands from Moltke and King Wilhelm. In the end, the Germans lost about 5,000 of their soldiers, while the French fared better with only 3,600 casualties. Neither side was willing to turn this into a more serious battle. On the one hand, Moltke was rightfully afraid the French were planning some kind of counterattack while his forces were still only arriving. On the other side, Bazaine ignored Leboeuf's warnings from the days after the battles at Spicheren and Froeschwiller-Woerth that the French commanders had to shift into a counteroffensive when the Germans first showed signs of faltering. Once again, had they done something more than staying put, the French may have thrown a wrench into Moltke's plan. Instead, Bazaine remained inactive, even stopping any further retreats. It seemed like he lost the will to fight, almost as if it was out of spite toward Napoleon.

Having wasted more than a week on personal squabbles and day-to-day insignificances, such as the cutlery supply of his cantinas, Bazaine was finally on the move. On August 15th, the marshal finally started his retreat, transporting his remaining troops over to the western banks of the Moselle. Even then, his action was sluggish, as he paused the retreat in the early hours of the 16th to deal with the confusion created by the withdrawal. All the while, the French retreat was under constant harassment by the Prussian cavalry, meaning that the wounded troops and supply transports needed armed escorts, which only added to the difficulties of evacuating from Metz. Luckily for Bazaine, the Prussians were not yet fully in striking distance, as only parts of the Second Army were near enough. In fact, on August 15th, Moltke was enacting a pivoting maneuver centered around several corps of the First and Second Army near Metz while crossing the Moselle with his flanks. It was somewhat of a calculated risk, as at that moment, the entire Prussian invasion was susceptible to a French counteroffensive. Nevertheless, the Prussian *Generalstab* saw little incentive among the French for such actions and decided to gamble.

On August 16th, the retreating French forces came into the firing range of the Prussian artillery, further scaring Bazaine. He thought that Moltke was trying to cut him off from Metz, which still had its garrison and formidable fortified defenses, as well as trying to encircle him on the open field. Thus, instead of continuing his retreat, he entrenched himself at Gravelotte, keeping an open road to Metz. That was exactly what Moltke wanted, as he sought to prevent the French from establishing a new defensive line at Châlons, which would put both the Meuse and the Marne Rivers between the two forces. Furthermore, Châlons was the place where the remains of MacMahon's troops and a French reserve army were gathering. Despite that, Moltke still didn't plan a serious confrontation with the French, as the Prussian troops were still gathering and positioning around Metz and the Moselle.

Regardless of Moltke's plans, the freedom of action exhibited by middle-ranking officers once again drew the Prussians into an unwanted battle. In the early morning of August 16th, commander of the Prussian III Corps ordered an attack on the French positions alongside the road to Verdun, despite being warned that the enemy had massed considerable troops there. A Prussian commander thought these were mere rearguards of the retreating French Army and wanted to separate it from the presumed main bulk farther west. He ordered his two divisions to take Mars-la-Tour, a village alongside the road. Unwittingly, he engaged four French corps, with the added trouble of having no nearby reinforcements available to him for hours. The French, on the other hand, had the entire Army of the Rhine nearby. Thus, the Battle of Mars-la-Tour should have been an easy victory for the French.

The start of the skirmish certainly signaled as much, as the French quickly drove off the Prussian attack. The Prussian division was smashed by French superior numbers and rifles. The initial breakdown was only avoided by the Prussian artilleries' suppressing fire, which stopped the French from exploiting their early advantage. As midday closed in, the French were in a perfect position to wipe out the entire III Corps, even exploiting the situation for a much serious counteroffensive, as the Prussian forces were divided and vulnerable. The French corps generals were indecisive, waiting for an order from Bazaine. Among them was the recently demoted Leboeuf, who now urged the marshal not to squander their advantage. Yet, Bazaine forbade them from acting. He was only concerned with maintaining an open road back to Metz. Nevertheless, by the early afternoon, the single Prussian corps remained under heavy fire, taking massive casualties. In a desperate act, the Prussian commander ordered his cavalry on a suicide flanking attack to relieve some pressure from the infantry. Despite delaying the order for a while, the Prussian cavalry finally attacked. By utilizing the hilly terrain, they managed to surprise part of the French artillery line, disrupting and panicking them. More than half of them died, yet the horsemen managed to buy the rest of the III Corps some time.

This act only reinforced Bazaine's defensive disposition, going as far as to personally ride to Leboeuf and stopping his independent action of cutting off the Prussian line of retreat. Instead, the marshal ordered him to retreat to Gravelotte. As the afternoon dragged on, the

Prussian artillery batteries exhibited their independence, amassing behind the III Corps on their own. Their potent fire kept the French at bay long enough for the Prussian X Corps to arrive and support their exhausted comrades. During the late afternoon, some local counterattacks were attempted by the French, but they proved futile, as, by then, the Prussian artillery was massed enough to rip them apart. As dusk fell, the battle began to settle into a stalemate. In the early evening, as night was falling, the Prussians tried one last attack, and for a while, chaos expanded throughout the battleground, yet with the cover of darkness, the hostilities fizzled out.

A painting of the Prussian cavalry charge at Mars-la-Tour.
Source: https://commons.wikimedia.org/wiki/File:Battleof_Rezonville.jpg

Tactically speaking, the Battle of Mars-la-Tour was a draw, as both sides had similar losses, around sixteen thousand men each. Yet, strategically, it was another loss for the French. Under concealment of night, they withdrew to Gravelotte, yielding the road to Verdun to the Prussians. The Army of the Rhine was slowly being cut off from its retreat lines. Furthermore, despite losing the same number of troops, the Prussians were able to brush them off because of their numerical superiority. Only adding to the inconspicuous disaster was the fact that Bazaine had all the prospects for an easy win. The French could have struck a serious blow to Prince Friedrich Karl and the Second Army, all with the strategic possibility of retreating to Verdun and further stretch the Prussian forces that still had to deal with Metz and its garrison. On an even grander scale, Mars-la-Tour proved to be politically decisive. Any chance of Austria, Italy, or Denmark joining France in the war was now gone. No one would join a war effort that seemed destined to fail.

The next day, Marshal Bazaine shocked his subordinates by ordering a retreat to Plappeville, one of Metz's outlying fortifications. He argued that the withdrawal toward Verdun was too dangerous at the moment, yet most of his generals claimed there was ample possibility to slip away, if not to Verdun then to the northwest and Sedan. Regardless, Bazaine chose Metz, redeploying by the late afternoon to a ridge above Gravelotte, blocking the western approach to the city. Simultaneously, Moltke and Friedrich Karl moved their troops in a swinging motion, cutting off the line between Verdun and Metz and finalizing their encirclement of the French Army. The prince sent numerous patrols, making sure that were no French fighting forces behind their back. To his relief, he found only stragglers and deserters. With that, the battle lines finally shifted 180 degrees. Initially, the French fought on the west and the Germans on the east side of the front, while at Mars-la-Tour, the former fought on the north and the latter on the south. After August 17th, the Prussians' backs were turned west, toward Paris, while the French had their backs turned east, toward Metz and ultimately Berlin. Regardless, Moltke decided to make his decisive action properly organized, and he reined in his commanders, including Steinmetz, massing his troops in encircling lines.

At the same time, Napoleon III arrived at Châlons, where he met with MacMahon and what was dubbed the Army of Châlons. Upon talking with Marshal MacMahon and the few officers that were present, they agreed that this army should take defensive positions around Paris, hoping to make the Prussian siege of the capital as painful as possible. Yet, the empress and the government in Paris persuaded the weak-willed Napoleon to change his mind, almost ordering him to utilize the last available French fighters for a diversion that would relieve some pressure off Bazaine and the Army of the Rhine. That decision was yet another nail in the coffin. While Napoleon sank deeper into depression, Bismarck visited the front line. He was exalted that the Prussian forces were winning and setting the pace of the war, but he felt slightly appalled by the general's brutality. They were too willing to sacrifice their own men, including Bismarck's son, Herbert, who was wounded in the cavalry charge at Mars-la-Tour. Such brutality would shine through the very next day when the Germans finally attacked Bazaine.

Unlike previous *positions magnifique*, Gravelotte wasn't as strong. The left wing could utilize hills, ravines, and the Moselle to anchor the French defense. In contrast, the French right wing lacked any natural obstacles. That weakness could've been offset by adding additional artillery and troops, something Bazaine ignored. Making his position worse, the marshal put his weakest corps there while positioning his reserves hours away from that vulnerable spot. The battle began on the morning of August 18th, when Prince Friedrich Karl ordered his units to advance. Moltke was determined to utilize more finesse than in previous battles, which was possible this time around, as this clash was anticipated and planned for by both sides. It was also the largest battle of the war, with about 200,000 German soldiers fighting against about 160,000 French troops, with hundreds of cannons on both sides. Despite that, Friedrich Karl initially thought that the forces in the French center were merely a rearguard, so he suspected that Bazaine was retreating to Metz. Thus, he ordered the bulk of the Second Army to engage in a frontal attack. Luckily, Moltke was present at the battlefield and realized the prince's error. He ordered the assault to spread out, sending additional corps to his left wing to help envelop the weak French right wing.

While the Prussian troops were still repositioning, a single division at the center made the first unauthorized attack at the center. They struck at heavily fortified French positions and quickly began to falter. At that crucial moment, General Steinmetz once again disobeyed Moltke. Instead of cutting off the assault, he ordered additional corps to it, taking command of units that were assigned to the Second Army and overreaching his authority. The attack quickly turned into yet another unnecessary slaughter of Prussian soldiers, especially as the flanking corps still weren't ready to attack. Steinmetz sent wave after wave of men, none of whom made any progress. King Wilhelm, who was present at the battlefield, was displeased by the number of his soldiers fleeing the assault, calling them cowards. This only further angered Moltke, who saw that the entire attack was a wasteful massacre of Prussian troops, all of whom he deemed heroes.

A 1910 painting depicting the Prussian infantry advance at Gravelotte.
Source: https://commons.wikimedia.org/wiki/File:Ernst_Zimmer_-_Das_Lauenburgische_J%C3%A4ger-Bataillon_Nr._9_bei_Gravelotte.jpg

The French once again failed to exploit the initial Prussian mistake. By the early afternoon, the Prussian left wing engaged, making any counterattack impossible. All the while, the German artillery masses shredded through the defenses, tearing down French morale along with Frenchmen. By the late afternoon, the fortunes of battle were turning. The French right wing demanded reinforcements and supplies, both of which Bazaine refused. The Prussian troops made a wide flanking maneuver, yet as the French fire was silenced by the artillery, they assumed the French were driven out. Thus, the Prussian left wing attacked prematurely, without fully completing the flanking maneuver, adding to the number of unnecessary casualties. Their initial push was easily repulsed by the Chassepot. Nevertheless, they soon regrouped and properly flanked the French, whose right wing began to collapse. As night closed in, the left-center of the Army of the Rhine also began to crumble under the pressure.

Throughout the afternoon, the general commanding the reserve units tried to gain permission from Bazaine to reinforce the obviously failing right wing, but he could not obtain it. The marshal simply mumbled about defensive positions without issuing many direct orders. To his subordinates, he seemed genuinely uninterested in a fight. Without committing his reserves, Bazaine wasted thirty thousand of his elite soldiers and more than one hundred guns, all while his positions were cracking. Seeing that development, Steinmetz wanted to strike the final blow himself. Indulged by his old friend, Wilhelm I, he ordered a renewed attack on the center. Once again, this led to a senseless slaughter, as the French mitrailleuses continued to mow them down. Moltke remained silent, unable to challenge his king. With the shroud of night, the French right wing finally collapsed. Something similar happened with Steinmetz's frontal assault. Regardless, the battle was coming to an end.

An 1881 painting depicting French casualties at their defensive positions at Gravelotte.
Source: *https://commons.wikimedia.org/wiki/File:AlphonseNeuvilleFriedhofSaint-PrivatL1100806_(2).jpg*

In a strategic sense, the Battle of Gravelotte was a clear French defeat. The Army of the Rhine was enclosed, now cut off even from retreat toward Sedan. The men could only find shelter at Metz, and they didn't have enough food or ammunition to hold off for a long time. Yet, due to the reckless Prussian command, it wasn't a total defeat. King Wilhelm himself didn't see the battle as much of a victory, as the Prussian Army lost about twenty thousand men, while the French losses were only at twelve thousand, including four thousand captives. Had the battle been under Moltke's undisputed command, the Germans would have likely lost fewer men and would have inflicted a much more decisive defeat. Regardless, it is vital to point out that the victory, no matter how flawed, was won by Prussian maneuvering and its superior artillery, which was responsible for roughly 70 percent of French casualties. With the effective loss of the entire Army of the Rhine, France was teetering toward total defeat in the war.

Chapter 6 – Waving the White Flag: The String of French Defeats

After the Battle of Gravelotte, the Franco-Prussian War transformed into a fox hunt for a while, leaving the conflict void of any larger clashes. While the Prussians were chasing the French, the action of their enemies confused everyone, as they lacked any common sense.

In the days after Gravelotte, Bazaine retreated to Metz with an army of 140,000 strong, including roughly 12,000 wounded. That move was essentially a death trap, as the city was already lacking provisions for its garrison and about seventy thousand citizens. Additional mouths were hard to feed, and even water supplies became an issue. The Moselle wasn't the best source of water, as it was somewhat polluted. The only real chance for survival of the now renamed Army of Metz was a breakthrough. Yet, Bazaine was set in his lethargy, which began to spread among his subordinate officers as well. Two lackluster attempts were made on August 26th and 31st, but the Prussians easily pushed them back. The lack of vigor and will is the only explanation to why a fighting force of about 130,000 French soldiers and hundreds of guns were unable to break through the thinned Prussian siege lines. In fact, on August 31ˢᵗ, the initial clash pitted eight French divisions against a single Prussian division. Utilizing Metz's forts to bog down the Prussian redeployment, a successful breakthrough was more than possible.

French cavalrymen photographed in Metz.
Source: https://commons.wikimedia.org/wiki/File:CuirassiersMetz1870.jpg

In that scenario, Bazaine had a multitude of possible actions. His Army of Metz could've retreated to the Vosges and threatened Prussian supply lines, or he could have pushed north to Sedan and unite with MacMahon. Or he could have moved in a direction to threaten the flanks or rears of the advancing Prussian forces. Instead, Bazaine remained passive, certain that his breakthrough attempts would eventually fail. His officers quickly reconciled with such a fate, leaving their soldiers to slowly starve. Two attempted sorties only increased the number of wounded, compounding the issue. The marshal was later accused of treason for the entirety of his actions, possibly because he wished to see the Bonaparte regime fall. Though this remains a possibility or at least a partial reasoning behind some of his actions, the sources hint that his defeatist attitude was the far more plausible culprit. He simply lost his will to fight and spread a similar attitude to his own troops as well.

Communication between Metz and Paris was mostly cut off, leaving MacMahon in the dark. He had hints that Bazaine would try to break out and head toward Sedan; thus, he chose to move his army northward from Châlons. He wanted to remain near Paris to help in its defense, yet the orders from Paris were clear—help Bazaine. Not wishing to tarnish his own reputation by abandoning the Army of Metz, MacMahon complied. The only solace he had was the promotion to *general en chef,* now officially outranking the emperor himself. The promotion came from Paris, where Empress Eugénie became more of a monarch than Napoleon III, who was only sinking further into his depression.

While Bazaine's inactivity played right into Moltke's hand once again, MacMahon's actions were puzzling to him. He was unsure of the *general en chef's* intentions, fearing they may be some kind of feint to draw out and prolong Prussian movement in a wild goose chase while Paris strengthened its defenses. His keen strategic mind was aware that moving the last French fighting force to Sedan, and even worse, taking the northern route to aid the forces in Metz, was a ludicrous move destined to fail. Yet, after his scouts had encountered no other kind of activity from the French for several days, Moltke decided to gamble and commit to chasing MacMahon.

In the prior days, Moltke reformed his armies. Prince Friedrich Karl was the given overarching command of the siege of Metz, including control over the Second Army. This naturally infuriated Steinmetz, but by mid-September, he was relieved of duty and sent to Prussia to become the governor of Posen (modern Poznan). The besieging force numbered around 150,000 men. However, a large chunk of the Second Army was detached from it and given to Crown Prince Albert of Saxony. This became the Fourth Army or the Army of the Meuse. It had around ninety thousand men and was tasked to move westward toward Verdun. On its left wing was the Third Army, which was still under the command of Friedrich Wilhelm; it numbered about 130,000, and it was moving toward the Meuse and the Marne Rivers, reaching the latter on August 24th. It is worth noting that by that time, more than 100,000 fresh conscripts arrived from Prussia, replacing their losses and even increasing the German fighting force. Worryingly for France, even more troops were still being formed in Prussia.

The freedom to gather and move such large reinforcements was partially aided by the total failure of the French Navy. It outnumbered the Prussian fleet roughly ten to one, and at the start of the war, there were plans to use it for a naval invasion or at least for disruptive actions along the Prussian coastline. However, French ships constantly lacked coal, and their officers lacked familiarity with the seas there. No German or Danish seamen wanted to aid them with their knowledge. Also, hauling coal from France was exhausting, and the Prussians outfitted their shorelines with formidable Krupp cannons that outranged any French naval gun. Overall, they were unable to do anything to jeopardize the Prussian home front. Additionally, as the crisis on the land expanded, what little marines were available for any naval operations were recalled to serve under MacMahon. By September, the French had ceased all naval operations and returned the ships to their harbor, as even their ill-attempted economic blockade proved inefficient.

Regardless, by August 26th, two German armies began their chase. Moltke's bold decision was also playing in favor of Bismarck's plans and political needs. While prior to Gravelotte, Prussia faced little international pressure, its great victory and France's blunder started to create a commotion. The Italians and Austrians became openly concerned with the future of France, while Britain began to ponder the balance of European power. Even the long neutral Russians began to watch with unease at the development in the west. All of the major powers feared that Prussia might fully dismember France. Their restlessness caused politicians in Berlin to worry about the possibility that some kind of unified action from Britain, Russia, Austria, and Italy might be aimed at restraining Prussia. Thus, Bismarck was aware a quick victory was needed to prevent other powers from interfering. So, the chancellor was more than pleased with the possibility of destroying the remaining French forces in a decisive battle. The only hole in his plans was the possibility of capturing the emperor himself, which would prevent Napoleon from arranging a quick peace the Prussians needed.

The first contacts between the pursuing German forces and MacMahon's troops occurred on August 29th, as a French corps and a Prussian corps collided near Buzancy, some twenty-five miles (forty kilometers) south of Sedan. It was clear the two armies were on a collision course, as Moltke planned to catch the French on the left bank of the Meuse. The initial clash at Buzancy lasted for a while before the French corps retreated north, taking up positions at Beaumont, which was twice as close to Sedan. Early on the next day, the Germans managed to surprise the tired French troops there, routing them rather quickly. The clash was short-lived, leaving the French with a staggering 7,500 casualties, while Germans lost only 3,500 men. The rest of the French Corps scattered farther north to Mouzon, where the main body of MacMahon's army was trying to cross on the left bank of the Meuse.

The skirmish at Beaumont signaled to MacMahon that the Prussians were advancing on him from the south as well from the east. Continuing his river crossing would be suicide. Furthermore, he was cut off both from Metz and Paris, and he could only retreat northward to Sedan, which had an outdated 17th-century fort on the right bank of the Meuse, near the Belgian border. He had two possible options. Either he would attempt a last stand at Sedan or cross into Belgium, knocking his army out of the war as international law stipulated. Without much pondering, he ordered his troops toward the old fort. Moltke was also aware of the situation. Thus, he ordered the Third Army, which was on the left bank of the Meuse, to move directly toward Sedan, while the Army of the Meuse was ordered to encircle the fort from the east and north, effectively cutting off MacMahon from Belgium. With that, the Army of Châlons would be trapped, surrounded by the Germans on all sides.

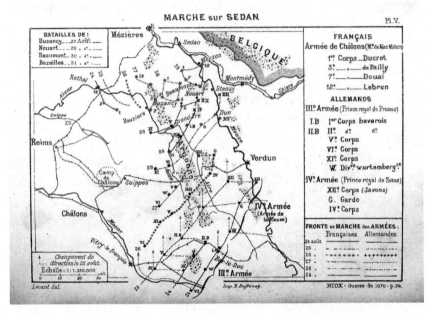

A map depicting Prussians (blue) advancing toward the French (red), forcing them toward Sedan.
Source: BrunoLC, CC0, via Wikimedia Commons
https://commons.wikimedia.org/wiki/File:Arm%C3%A9e_de_Ch%C3%A2lons_-_Marche_sur_Sedan.jpg

Having little time to prepare his positions, MacMahon acted too conservatively, arranging his troops in a tight triangle in front of Sedan. This was erroneous, as the French troops would then be perfectly gathered to be torn to shreds by the Prussian artillery while having nowhere to retreat to apart from Sedan. Furthermore, the outdated fortifications no longer provided sufficient support or defense. Even the Meuse offered little help. The German guns on the left bank of the river could still fire at the French troops massed on the right bank in front of the castle. For Moltke, it was the perfect trap, and even the French generals were aware of that. Moltke just needed a bit of time to finalize his encirclement maneuvers.

However, the battle once again prematurely started by an overzealous middle-ranked officer. In the early hours of September

1st, a single Bavarian corps engaged the southernmost tip of French defenses. Since the rest of the German troops were still not positioned for a fight, the Bavarians were repulsed, and their initial attack seemed to be yet another waste of German lives. Regardless, they were quickly reinforced as the rest of the German units continued to assume their given positions. As they arrived, the artillery batteries began firing upon the French positions, slowly massing and taking favorable positions for a bombardment. In those early hours of the battle, just as it was turning into full-blown combat, MacMahon was seriously wounded. Shrapnel from an artillery shell lacerated his leg, making him unable to command. He made General Auguste Ducrot, a veteran and trusted officer, the commander-in-chief. However, this was almost immediately disputed by the recently appointed General Emmanuel Wimpffen, who held higher seniority over the officers. This led to confusion, as for a while, the French troops weren't sure who held the reins. Eventually, Wimpffen took general command, but disorder persisted.

As the Prussian envelopment continued, their artillery assumed positions on the slopes overlooking the dug-in French troops. It wasn't long before their overlapping fire began to pummel the defenses and the defenders. Both began to crumble under such pressure, for about seven hundred artillery guns rained shells upon them. By noon, the German artillery was capable of shattering every French attempt of counterattack, battery fire, and even the mitrailleuse nest in a matter of minutes. Their fire, precision, and coordination were almost textbook, far beyond what should have been possible in the chaos of battle. Yet, they had superior positions as well as guns, while the French had no way to reach them nor disrupt their fire. Furthermore, by midday, the defenders were more or less left without any support of their own artillery, as it was either destroyed or abandoned. Eventually, the German batteries were able to relocate to different positions, searching for the best angle at a target, with several batteries aiming at a single spot. Thus, shells rained from various overlapping directions, making finding suitable shelter almost impossible for the French.

With such unbearable conditions and with French units slowly disintegrating, both Wimpffen and Ducrot realized they needed a breakthrough. They organized two almost simultaneous attempts, one toward the west and one toward the southeast. These attempts weren't coordinated or properly organized, so they failed miserably. The Prussian artillery broke them easily, leaving infantrymen to finish off the French. All the while, the French units continued to dissolve, with chaotic masses of soldiers trying to seek refuge inside the fort. All the cracks and gaps left by them were quickly filled with the German units, which exploited every opportunity to the fullest.

As the afternoon dragged on, the French forces were nearing total collapse. They had about seventeen thousand casualties, with another twenty-one thousand taken as prisoners. The Germans had lost nine thousand men altogether. Seeing that there was no real way out, Napoleon III conferred with his generals. All but Wimpffen were in favor of surrender, and the emperor complied. A white flag was erected on the walls of Sedan, while Napoleon's adjutant rode under one toward the Prussian headquarters. He was carrying a letter of surrender to King Wilhelm I, who was present there together with Bismarck and Moltke. Exaltation spread amongst the Prussian camp, and Bismarck accepted the surrender in the name of his monarch, appointing Moltke for further negotiations of the French surrender.

A painting depicting Bismarck's (right) stern talk with Napoleon III (left) after the Battle of Sedan.

Having muscled himself as the commander of the Army of Châlons, it was up to Wimpffen to hammer out the capitulation terms with Moltke. The French general pleaded for leniency, asking for an "honorable capitulation." Moltke refused. He wouldn't allow the French troops to march away with their equipment and military honors. It would be ludicrous, as they were sure to fight them again. Bismarck shared his views. To assure Wimpffen's compliance with total capitulation, Moltke showed him a diagram of Prussian battery positions, stating that a force of over 200,000 men and 700 guns would continue their attack tomorrow morning if the French refused. Wimpffen accepted immediately. To protect his reputation, he also forced other French generals to sign a note of compliance to the terms of surrender. Only Napoleon III didn't sign. Instead, he rode to Wilhelm I the next morning, imploring him personally for leniency. Before he was able to present his case, Bismarck gave him a longwinded lesson, leaving the emperor without any words for the king.

In a matter of hours, the capitulation was signed, adding another 83,000 French prisoners, raising the total tally to 104,000. The entire Army of Châlons, 130,000 strong, was removed from the war. The emperor was captured, and the road to Paris was undefended. France was in a dreadful position overall, as no proper fighting force was available to an already wavering government in Paris. The Prussians' success was paid with only about nine thousand German casualties. Those losses were lessened by the fact that tens of thousands of Chassepot rifles and hundreds of artillery guns were now in German hands.

The captured French conscripts were slowly shipped toward Prussia and were held in rather abysmal conditions. It was only upon seeing those columns that the defenders at Metz realized no relief was coming. Bazaine ordered no more sorties, only small-scale scavenging missions. The Army of Metz slowly withered away as starvation and sickness began taking their toll. Such inactivity was a relief to Moltke, who sent his two armies from Sedan to Paris. They reached the French capital on September 15th. The Army of the Meuse began spreading around the city from the north, while the Third Army wrapped around it from the south. By September 19th, Paris was cut off, surrounded by roughly 240,000 German troops. Regardless, the city wasn't in much danger from a full-blown attack. It bolstered strong defensive forts, which were aided by makeshift barricades and fortifications and covered by more than 1,300 guns. Furthermore, it had a garrison of about 400,000 to 450,000 men; however, only less than 100,000 were trained soldiers. Others were members of the national guard, meaning they lacked discipline or proper training. Even so, together, they proved enough of a deterrent to the Germans but were unable to mount any serious breakthrough.

With the sieges of Paris and Metz, the war entered a military stalemate. The French were unable to mount any kind of counteroffensive; even the forces gathered in the rest of the country were momentarily lacking in training and supplies. On the other hand, the German forces were strung out, unable to storm the formidable forces that tied down almost all of their fighting capacities. Additionally, both sides had troubles with supplies, most notably food. The besieged French forces were in a slightly worse position, yet the Germans weren't faring much better, as the countryside they were encamped on was quickly depleted. The worsening autumn weather only added to the troubles, as illnesses began plaguing both sides. Thus, for a while, the war shifted back to being a political issue more than a military one. Bismarck was back in the spotlight.

Despite the major victories and more than favorable odds, securing peace wouldn't be easy. Bismarck and Moltke believed that Napoleon would slip away from Sedan, allowing them to pursue a quick peace. Instead, he was captured. In a matter of days, the Second French Empire crumbled. On September 4th, when news of Sedan reached the capital, riots erupted almost immediately. The masses wanted to oust the Bonaparte regime. Politicians Léon Gambetta and Jules Favre, backed by General Louis Trochu, proclaimed a provisional government. The so-called Government of National Defense was plagued by numerous political issues. First of all, its leaders weren't properly elected, and almost immediately, it split into two opposing factions. On one side were the moderates, representing the rural population and better-off social classes, who were in favor of gaining peace as quickly as possible. On the other side were the radicals, which mostly contained the poorer urban working classes, who were imbued with nationalism and antimonarchism. They wanted a "maximum war"; in other words, they wanted the Germans to pay in blood.

An 1860s photograph of Favre
Source: *https://commons.wikimedia.org/wiki/File:Jules_Favre_1865_Nadar.jpg*

Gambetta
Source: *https://commons.wikimedia.org/wiki/File:L%C3%A9on_Gambetta_by_Leg%C3%A9,_Paris.png*

The provisional government tried to find some middle ground, but that proved difficult. The rural population wanted nothing but peace, while the proletarian movement in Paris began campaigning for *La Commune*. They wanted to establish a new order of shared wealth and property led by local communes. In short, it was the first actual, active seeds of communist ideology in political life. The new government had to suppress such movements, leaving Paris in almost constant chaos of protests and riots. The commotion and the advancing Prussian troops prompted the republican government to split itself. Trochu, its provisional head and commander of the Parisian forces, stayed in the capital with Gambetta, while Favre and a "government delegation" went to Tours on September 13th. There, they would organize the rest of France in the upcoming war effort.

The commotion caused by the fall of the empire caused Bismarck substantial problems. He had hoped to finish the war before the neutral nations stepped in to intervene, but he wasn't going to settle for mere monetary settlement. He demanded Alsace and Lorraine from the provisional government. It was to be a punishment for the war as well as past humiliations that the French had caused the German people. Furthermore, Bismarck's demands were backed up by the Prussians' historical claim on the regions, as they were once part of the Holy Roman Empire. Favre refused such peace offers, claiming that France wouldn't yield an inch of its lands to the Germans. His counteroffer was a large indemnity and part of the French fleet; he was even willing to negotiate about ceding some colonies outside Europe. Bismarck wasn't interested. Thus, the two sides were locked in the talks, neither willing to compromise on their stance.

With both Favre and Bismarck stubbornly set in their ways, they tried to find other political means to achieve them. France sent their ambassadors around Europe and talked with foreign representatives in Paris. They tried to persuade other nations to put pressure on the Germans to accept a less favorable peace treaty. In the cases of Russia and Italy, the French diplomats tried to tempt them with territorial gains in the Balkans and Rome, respectively. In the cases of Austria and Britain, they dangled the threatened balance of power if Prussia became too powerful. However, they weren't able to make any real allies, apart from vague support from Italy. The French diplomatic position was hardened by the lack of a strong and unified government, leaving many to wonder if the current leaders even had control over the nation. Furthermore, some of the opponents of the provisional government actually traveled around the continent, spreading the "red scare" of impending revolutions, while members of earlier dynasties, like the Bourbons and Orléans, loomed around the border, waiting for their opportunity.

Of course, Bismarck wasn't going to sit around and wait. Prussia also used diplomacy to maintain the neutrality of other European nations. However, his main concern was how to force the French to peace. Being a keen politician, he began plotting on two fronts. On the one hand, he tried negotiating with Bazaine. The marshal was offered liberation from Metz to lead a counter-coup with Prussian support, with the aim of either reestablishing the Bonaparte regime in some kind of capacity or even establishing his own personal dictatorship. These topics were also brought to the empress, who had escaped to Britain in early September, and to Napoleon himself. However, these bore no fruit, as both Bazaine and the Bonapartes wanted too much leeway and separation from the Germans. Nevertheless, Bazaine's willingness to negotiate in such a capacity and his refusal to recognize the new republican government just added to the image of his betrayal of the French people.

Bismarck's other front was trying to negotiate a nationwide election across France, including the return of Alsace and Lorraine, with the Government of National Defense. He hoped that these would provide a more stable and widely accepted government, one that would be able to accept Prussian demands. That offer was rebuffed, as it implied the continued German occupation of France.

Nevertheless, by declining to hold an election, regardless of Prussian participation in holding them, the provisional government's credibility was hurt. To some, it was a sign of yearning to hold power while disregarding the will of the people. As time passed, France was slowly losing its unity. Paris was experiencing increasing revolutionary fervor, which expanded, to some extent, to other major cities. The rural population, usually more monarchical orientated, began feeling too much exhaustion with the burden of war as well as resentment toward the republic. Overall, the government in Tours was losing its grip over France.

Political uncertainty quickly eroded the idea of a diplomatic solution to the war. By early October, it was clear that the war needed a more militaristic resolution. Both sides prepared for renewed combat operations, though the negotiations never fully stopped. Talks would be done with the sound of guns and rifles in the background.

Chapter 7 –The Last Stand: The Road to Peace and the End of the War

As the autumn began to take hold, the hostilities in the French countryside would resume. Taking advantage of the relative lull on the front line, the provisional government managed to gather some troops in the south. In contrast, the relative inactivity of the Parisian defenders allowed Moltke to detach several divisions under the command of Bavarian General Ludwig von der Tann to combat the new threat.

Moltke's military solution to a political stalemate was to actively search and destroy French relief armies, which had the added bonus of safeguarding the ongoing siege of Paris. Tann commanded the Bavarian I Corps and was aided by some Prussian infantry and cavalry divisions. It was a detachment roughly fifty thousand men strong, and it traveled south toward Orléans and the Loire River. Along the way, they met little resistance, mostly some local partisan troops. These kinds of troops plagued the entire German army. However, their actions were more a nuisance than a threat. Even some of the locals refused to help them, fearing Prussian retribution. Regardless of the irregular resistance, for the detached corps, the march southward was initially a welcome rest. Unlike the depleted surroundings of Paris, this region was largely intact, and the men managed to find plentiful supplies.

By October 9th, Tann's troops arrived just north of Orléans, where they were welcomed by a small French force under the command of General Joseph de La Motte-Rouge. Adding to the problems of numbers, most of the French soldiers were part of the national guard, meaning they had little to no training. Only a smaller number of them were properly trained; some had been recalled from their station in Rome, some were part of the French Foreign Legionnaires, and some were the scraps of the regular troops. The mostly untrained and inexperienced French corps was no match to the Germans. In the initial clash, they were quickly routed, while the Germans used their cavalry to flank them. Motte-Rouge tried to position his troops defensively at Orléans, but when they were engaged by the German artillery, they stood no chance. On October 11th, the French corps scrambled. Their losses were incomparable with the Germans, as no less than four thousand trained soldiers were killed or captured—exactly those troops France couldn't afford to lose. In contrast, the Germans lost maybe around nine hundred men.

Once Orléans was captured, Tann was faced with a problem. Pursuing the enemy wasn't an option, as more troops were gathering in much larger numbers farther south. If he ventured too far, he would be too exposed. The detached army already felt exposed, but Moltke rebuffed any ideas of retreat. Thus, the Germans began reinforcing their defenses at Orléans, arming themselves with Chassepots to better their defensive capabilities. They also gathered as much food as they could, plundering the region to prepare for the upcoming winter. These were sometimes masked by terms of "requisition," some vague deals that the French government would later cover with their expenses, or threat of violence. The pressure of war was spreading across France, which only added to the defeatist atmosphere. More and more peasants wanted nothing more than peace.

Moltke ordered Tann, who had been left to guard the forces besieging Paris, to suppress any organized resistance from the south. The Bavarian general complied, and after a few days, he dispatched some of his troops to some of the surrounding towns. Those were conquered relatively easily, as they were inadequately defended. To ensure collaboration, the Germans showed no mercy. They maimed prisoners, shot suspected partisans, and burned villages and towns to the ground. They even took civilians as hostages. After securing the region, Moltke then redirected Tann toward Tours. He was to follow the Loire to the second capital. There, Gambetta, who had managed to sneak out of Paris on a hot air balloon, was taking over control of the French war effort. It seemed Moltke and Bismarck wanted to finish the war before winter truly came and made the lives of their soldiers miserable.

However, the French weren't going to sit idly. General Louis Aurelle de Paladines was given command of Motte-Rouge's XV Corps, which was aided by newly gathered troops. That fighting force now numbered about sixty thousand soldiers, though most of them were still untrained national guardsmen whose discipline was almost nonexistent. Nevertheless, his force, if combined with other troops massing in the south, could possibly rise up to challenge Moltke's siege of Paris. To achieve that, Aurelle needed to take hold of defendable crossroads closer to the capital, where he could be safe while training his conscripts to become proper soldiers. The only real solution was to retake Orléans. Along with other remaining high-ranking officers, plans for that action were made, while Gambetta and his government worked hard to procure any kind of weapons and artillery from Europe and even from the US. Thus, these new French forces were being armed with thousands of Enfield, Remington, and Springfield rifles, as well as the reworked 1822 model muskets. These troops were also armed with repurposed naval guns.

While the new forces in the south of France were preparing to challenge the German forces on the battlefield, Bazaine's Army of Metz was slowly rotting away. His attempts to strike a bargain with Bismarck led nowhere, and even his troops caught wind of the covert communication. His own soldiers were either swept by apathy or anger, feeling personally betrayed. Even worse, many were suffering from starvation and diseases, and their equipment decayed in the bad weather, as most soldiers neglected to maintain them. By mid-October, this formidable fighting force was that only on paper, as in reality, it was unable for any concrete action. The soldiers began sustaining themselves on horse meat, but those supplies quickly ran out. Facing complete starvation and helped by the fact that the Prussians refused to take in more than a handful of deserters per day, Bazaine had no other way out than to surrender.

A picture of Prussian troops occupying one of Metz's forts after the French surrendered.
Source: https://commons.wikimedia.org/wiki/File:Beato,_Felice_A._-_Eine_von_Deutschen_besetzte_Festung_in_Metz_nach_der_%C3%9Cbergabe_durch_General_Bazaine_(Zeno_Fotografie).jpg

On October 29th, the Army of Metz capitulated. Prince Friedrich Karl offered Bazaine a surrender with full military honors, allowing the French to exit the fort armed with banners and marching music. Bazaine refused, ordering his men to simply stack their deteriorated rifles and wait for the Germans to take them away. Furthermore, he willingly gave up all their flags and standards, another controversial act, as most units preferred them destroyed rather than captured by the enemy. Regardless of the shameful conclusion of the siege of Metz, where Bazaine literally ran away from his men, France, in the end, lost another 140,000 men, including thousands of much-needed officers, while also giving up roughly 600 guns and more than 200,000 rifles. The tally of captured French soldiers went up to about 250,000, including 4 marshals, 140 generals, and 10,000 officers. When the news broke, another wave of violent outbursts swept France, especially in the capital. Yet, Parisians also reverted to dark humor, joking that at least Bazaine and MacMahon had finally joined forces. Regardless of the rage and despair shared by the masses, Gambetta and the provisional government in Tours refused to back down. They were determined to continue the struggles with the troops they could muster in the south.

Upon realizing that he was outnumbered, Tann remained at Orléans, perhaps waiting for some reinforcements from Metz. However, the French weren't going to wait, and in early November, they began their march toward him. Their plan was to group all their forces, which would number more than 100,000, and envelop the Germans from the south and the west. Yet, unlike his French counterparts, Tann wasn't going to wait for them to arrive. He decided to gamble, taking twenty thousand of his soldiers and marching to meet Aurelle's corps of sixty thousand. He hoped his better-trained troops would be able to outmaneuver and outperform the unruly French recruits. On November 9th, the two forces collided at Coulmiers, some ten miles (seventeen kilometers) west of Orléans. Tann's initial guess proved right, as, despite their numerical advantage, the French were unable to breach his thin lines. Yet, with so few soldiers, the Germans were pinned down and too weak to attack even though they had the advantage. To make matters worse, they were being rained on by the French artillery, which, though improvised from naval guns, began employing some Prussian tactics.

Thus, it became a war of attrition, something Tann wasn't going to win. To prevent a major disaster, he yielded his position by nightfall, though he managed to repulse all French attacks.

A 1911 illustration of the French celebrating their victory at Coulmiers.
Source: *https://commons.wikimedia.org/wiki/File:Bataille_de_Coulmiers.jpg*

By the next day, Aurelle arrived at Orléans to find that the Germans had retreated completely. Tann withdrew north to Angerville, halfway between his former position and Paris. This angered Moltke, who soon removed him from his commanding post. He gave it to Grand Duke Friedrich of Mecklenburg-Schwerin and reinforced the army with several Prussian corps and divisions from the Second Army. By mid-November, the forces from Metz were redeployed, following vaccinations against smallpox, which had begun to plague the soldiers due to their filthy living conditions. This new defensive German line was spread from Troyes to Chartres, covered by roughly 150,000 soldiers. Their orders were to protect the besiegers of Paris from any French attacks from the southwest. Against them stood a divided French force with an additional three newly formed corps. Combined with irregular militia and partisans, the French Army had swollen up to about 250,000 men, though most of them were still untrained.

However, Aurelle had no intention of massing an offensive. Instead, he entrenched at Orléans, largely ignoring requests for action from Gambetta and his government in Tours. He reasoned that the troops needed to be trained to become a functional army capable of serious combat. The cold winter weather and snow also helped in his resolve to stay in the warmth of a city. Despite the promises of freeing Paris, which had been made by the provisional government, this action was sensible. After the losses of almost all of the regular army, the French forces could survive only by being defensive. On the other hand, Grand Duke Friedrich was largely unaware of how bad the shape of the French Army was. Thus, he split his forces into several defensive positions while marching toward the French XXI Corps stationed at Le Mans. It was a preemptive strike at a force of only thirty-five thousand men that could, at some point, possibly threaten the besiegers of Paris from the west. However, the commander of the French corps retreated without giving battle. By then, the French had finally managed to bypass the lack of intelligence-gathering missions of their cavalry, which had plagued them in the early stages of the war. Now, they were relying on partisans and locals to gather information on Prussian movements and positions.

Through that intelligence network, the leaders of the provisional government learned that yet another batch of Prussian reinforcements, under Prince Friedrich Karl, was arriving from Metz. Gambetta and his republican high command felt that an early strike was the only solution, as they still had some numerical superiority against the southern German armies. Their main fear was that it was only a matter of time before these German troops grouped and advanced to Tours. Thus, they forced Aurelle to act, despite his hesitations. He gathered his troops and pushed to Beaune-la-Rolande. It was just twenty-five miles (forty kilometers) northeast of Orléans and guarded by three Prussian brigades. They were only meant to be an early warning for an attack, not a real line of German defense. So, Aurelle felt his rowdy army of 60,000 men and 140 guns could take on 9,000 Prussians with half as much artillery.

The two sides clashed on November 28th, but the French failed to exploit their superiority in numbers. Their attacks were repulsed by a remarkably disciplined and stubborn Prussian defense. Realizing they had no reserves or much supplies, they waited for each French advance to get to less than two hundred yards away before opening precise fire. All the while, they endured heavy artillery bombardments and mitrailleuse fire. The untrained French recruits were no match to the well-trained battle-hardened Prussians, who broke off the French offensive by the end of the day. The disparity in the quality of troops is exemplified through the casualties at Beaune-la-Rolande. The Germans had only 850, while the French lost roughly 8,000 men in a battle where they outnumbered the enemies more than six to one.

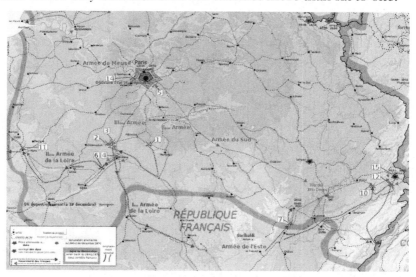

A map depicting rough army movements, positions, and the front lines from December 1870 to January 1871 (note – the French eastern border depicts Alsace and Lorraine as already part of Germany).

As if that loss wasn't enough for Aurelle and Gambetta, they proceeded with yet another attack. They sent another fresh corps at the German positions in Loigny, just north of Orléans, on December 2nd. This battle was between armies of equal size, roughly thirty-five thousand each, with both sides deployed in long skirmish lines on an open field that offered little protection against enemy fire or artillery shrapnel. A rather primitive shootout lasted the entire day, ending in a Prussian victory. The French lost seven thousand men, including captured, while the Germans suffered roughly four thousand casualties. It was a much closer call for the Germans simply because the open field suited the French longer-ranged rifles much better, yet they weren't able to exploit that. Furthermore, the harshness of winter caused troubles on both sides. However, the loss at Loigny proved to be the final straw for the greenhorns in the French Army.

Losing their morale and troubled by cold and hunger, the French were losing their willingness to oppose the Germans. Realizing that, Moltke ordered that that Orléans needed to be retaken. Prince Friedrich Karl amassed his troops and marched to it on December 3rd. The remaining French forces put up some resistance, yet they slowly yielded their positions under heavy artillery fire. The fight lasted for two days, but in the end, there wasn't much fight left in the French Army, and it descended into a chaotic rout. Aurelle's army split into two halves, one north and one south of the Loire. The French general ordered his troops to retreat farther south, leaving the ones north of the river on their own. In the end, Friedrich Karl recaptured Orléans, losing only about 1700 of his men in the process, while the French lost around 20,000, with 18,000 being prisoners. With that, any hope of relieving Paris was gone, and the provisional government retreated farther south, making Bordeaux its new informal capital.

Aurelle was relieved of duty, but the army remained split in two. The southern half was placed under the command of General Charles Bourbaki, who managed to slip away from Metz during the siege. His troops retreated toward Brogues. The northern part of the army was given to General Antoine Chanzy, who retreated toward Tours. At Beaugency, he tried to regroup his panicked soldiers. He gathered a disorganized army of about 100,000 men, with the bad weather only further hampering his efforts. These two factors made his army rather immobile, preventing him from moving his men to the left bank of the Loire and head over to reunite with Bourbaki. This allowed for a much smaller German force, with less than thirty thousand soldiers, to engage him in combat, which lasted for several days. Chanzy hoped that he could budge the Prussians by attacking them while waiting for some help from Bourbaki. By around December 10th, Moltke ordered Friedrich Karl to reinforce the advance on Beaugency. Realizing no help was coming, this left Chanzy with only the possibility of retreat. He headed west to Le Mans. The French managed to slip away mostly because the Germans weren't too keen on pursuing them, as cold weather and fatigue caught up with them. Similar conditions, aided with the demoralization from defeat, also bogged down Bourbaki's army. His soldiers simply refused to comply with the orders to move out. For a while, the southern front went quiet.

While the two sides clashed on the banks of the Loire, the Parisian front also lit up. Morale sank after the surrender of Metz, while the lack of supplies put added pressure on the Parisians. This prompted Trochu to act. After being informed of Aurelle's movements in late November, he and his generals planned a sortie on November 28th. It was supposed to strike southwest of Paris, simultaneously cutting off communications from Prussian headquarters in Versailles with the troops in the east of the city, while forming a bridge toward the troops advancing from the Loire and gathering supplies from the German besiegers. However, the engineers failed to mount pontoon bridges in time, derailing the attack and pushing it back to the 30th, giving time for the besiegers to prepare. The French tried to mask the main line of the sortie with a diversion, but the Prussians weren't fooled. They greeted their main attack at Villiers and Champigny, the southeastern outskirts of Paris, just south of the Marne. The battle lasted until December 4th, with the French clinging for longer than reasonable on Gambetta's vague promises of relief from the Loire.

The failed breakthrough cost the Parisians twelve thousand men, most of whom were the trained soldiers spearheading the assault; the number of trained men was already lacking among the defenders of Paris, which made this blow even harder to suffer. Regardless of the loss and creeping hunger, Paris refused to surrender. The provisional government refused as well, as Gambetta was resolute on continuing the fight, even after the Loire army was functionally knocked out of the war. This posed a new problem for the German occupiers, who had hoped these victories would finally force France into submission. On the one hand, Bismarck continuously worried about the neutral powers stepping in to rein in Prussia. On the other, prolonged war and the harsh winter continued to wear down Moltke's troops and supplies. The two of them argued and disagreed on what would be the proper solution for this French stubbornness.

Unusually, the politician argued for a more violent plan. Bismarck argued all they had to do was exert unbearable pressure on the civilians, forcing the provisional government to settle for his terms. Thus, he advocated relocating heavy guns and mortars to bombard Paris, regardless of the civilian population. His willingness to harm the French nation as a whole only increased due to the actions of French partisans and irregulars. Those forces, numbering maybe thirty thousand to forty thousand in total, weren't a match to the Prussian soldiers, but they constantly harassed the Prussians while they were on the move, disrupting supply lines by demolishing railways and bridges. This nuisance forced Moltke to separate about 100,000 men to guard shipments headed to the front lines. As soldiers had a hard time dealing with the elusive partisans, who were without uniforms, some simply began shooting at anyone even vaguely suspected of insurgent activities. It was a gruesome reprisal supported by Bismarck as another way of pressuring the French. Furthermore, he used reports of the partisans killing and torturing Prussian prisoners as more proof that they shouldn't show mercy to the civilians.

In contrast, Moltke was far less bloodthirsty. He wanted to starve out the French as they had done at Metz. He argued that transporting mortars and heavy guns, as well as their ammunition, would only add to the stress of resupplying the Prussian forces. Furthermore, he suggested that harming civilians en masse would only infuriate other countries, turning them firmly against Prussia. Not least, Moltke felt this kind of action wasn't very civilized or in the proper military and German spirit. Bismarck had no morality issues like those. He thought that brutality was justified to end the war before some unforeseen event, be it foreign intervention or reversal of battle fortunes, weakened Prussia's negotiating position. Bismarck dubbed this the "wartime political effort" (*Politik im Krieg*), where the military was working toward a political goal. This debate between the chancellor and field marshal was settled by the minister of war. Roon sided with Bismarck, swaying the king at the same time. The Prussians were to bombard Paris.

While the heavy guns were still being deployed, the Parisians attempted another breakthrough on December 21ˢᵗ. It was a sign of desperation, as it was now aimed toward the north, hoping to connect with the so-called Army of the North that was stationed in Lille. However, these thirty-five thousand men were soldiers only on paper, even according to their commanding officer, who characterized them as an unarmed and untrained group lacking proper officers. Their futility is further corroborated by the fact that the Prussians almost ignored their existence, satisfied with isolating them from the rest of France. Regardless, this sortie was rebuffed by the Germans with ease, while the Parisian defenders were starting to run low on sufficiently trained troops to send on such missions. Their low morale was soon to get even worse, for, by the last days of 1870, the Prussians finally deployed over seventy heavy guns and began their bombardment. Their primary targets were forts on the outskirts of Paris, which protected the city from invaders, but some shells managed to hit civilian targets, including hospitals, churches, schools, and private homes. Reports of noncombatant casualties began to seep in. However, German shells weren't a primary cause of civilian deaths. By January, up to four thousand citizens were dying weekly from starvation and cold.

Civilian parts of Paris that were damaged by Prussian artillery.
Source: https://commons.wikimedia.org/wiki/File:Braun,_Adolphe_(1811-1877)_-
Paris,_1871_-_St_Cloud,_La_place.jpg

While the Parisians suffered, Chanzy was entrenched at Le Mans with his army of about 100,000. He sent smaller regiments to harass the Second Army while the rest worked on fortifications. Along the way, the provisional government worked on reorganizing and resupplying its army, trying to increase its combat effectiveness. Moltke noticed that, and on New Year's Day, he ordered Prince Friedrich Karl to mobilize his army westward and deal a final strike to the Army of the Loire. The prince complied, gathering about seventy-three thousand of his men, and slowly advanced toward Le Mans, reaching it on January 10th. The men showed signs of fatigue over the long campaign and cold weather, so the initial German attack was rather uncoordinated and slow, allowing Chanzy's defenses to stave off the attackers for a day. Yet, the very next day, a bold advance surprised the inexperienced national guard regiments, causing panic and routing them. Once it began, Chanzy couldn't stop it. His soldiers were cold, wet, hungry, and sleepless, lacking any will to fight. The army virtually disintegrated, and the fighting broke off on January 12th. Chanzy and a small part of his troops managed to slip away. According to some estimations, he lost about twenty-five thousand men, both in casualties and prisoners, but up to twice as many deserted during the retreat. Regardless of how many men he retained under his command, that group ceased to be an effective fighting force. Soldiers abandoned much of their arms and ammunition, and morale was at an all-time low.

With Chanzy's demise and all Parisian breakout attempts failing, Gambetta turned his attention to the eastern theater of the war. By late December, he ordered Bourbaki's army to march toward Dijon, where a single Baden Corps was holding the city. Gambetta's idea was to strike the Prussian flank from the southeast, in the region between Dijon and Belfort, and hit the German supply lines. It was a reasonable last attempt at doing anything, especially since the small Army of the Vosges operated in the region. It was led by the famous Giuseppe Garibaldi, an old Italian revolutionary general, and consisted mostly of foreign volunteers, for example, Poles, Irish, Spanish, Americans, and, of course, Italians. These were usually somewhat experienced and trained men, but the unit lacked overall cohesion and discipline, with too many internal squabbles and debates. The volunteer army was operational since early November, with no more than twenty thousand men, but it made little impression on the course of the war. Yet, if that force was to unite and cooperate with Bourbaki's 110,000 men, together, they could seriously threaten the German rear.

Of course, Moltke was aware of that; thus, he formed a new German "Army of the South" from three Prussian corps and sent them in pursuit. The goal was to destroy France's last remnants of a field army. However, Bourbaki proved to be less of a threat than originally expected. His army advanced quite slowly, encumbered with supply issues, demoralization, and the cold. Regardless, the German corps holding the city withdrew without a fight in late December and began its retreat eastward. This was done because the primary task of the Badenese was to safeguard the siege of Belfort, a fortified town on the southern edges of the Vosges. Holding ground against a numerically superior enemy at Dijon, which was more than 80 miles (128 kilometers) west of Belfort, seemed unwise, as the men were far from any possible reinforcements and were vulnerable to encirclement. Thus, the Germans rolled all the way back to the Lisaine River and the fortified town of Héricourt, with the French slowly trailing behind them. The hesitation to engage the Baden Corps infuriated Bourbaki's superiors, and it made the Germans question if he was even going to relieve the siege of Belfort at all.

Regardless, the two sides finally clashed when the French attacked on January 15th. By then, Héricourt was fortified by the Badenese. The attackers crossed the frozen river that separated the two sides, and a three-day battle ensued, filled with heavy fighting, artillery exchanges, and harsh weather. The French had some limited success at certain points, taking parts of the German outer posts, but the defenders gave stiff resistance to their advances. By the end of the 17th, Bourbaki disengaged, losing about 8,000 men, while the Baden Corps suffered about 1,600 casualties. The French "eastern army" remained functional, yet with the German Army of the South approaching, it wasn't going to pose much of a threat anymore.

It was becoming obvious even to the fiercest French proponents of a defiant resistance that the war was lost. Trochu, who corresponded with Moltke about surrendering in early January, agreed upon a last desperate sortie on January 19th, but that attempt failed like the others, just adding to French casualty numbers. The very next day, Paris descended into riots, with the workers gathering on the streets, demanding the formation of communes and the removal of Trochu. They even began showing signs of distrust toward the republic. Such developments finally pushed Favre to travel to Versailles on January 23rd to begin negotiations with Bismarck. On January 26th, they signed an armistice, officially ending the hostilities on January 28th. The treaty stipulated that Paris had to surrender, giving up both its armaments and fortifications; in return, the Germans would immediately send in rations. Afterward, France had until February 19th to elect a national assembly, which would then ratify peace on German terms. If the assembly refused, the Prussians would descend upon the disarmed and exposed French nation.

The last remnants of the French Army surrendering their arms at the Swiss border.
Source: https://commons.wikimedia.org/wiki/File:Arm%C3%A9e-Bourb-en-Suisse.jpg

Thus, for most of the French, the war ended on January 28th, 1871, yet Favre and Gambetta still had illusions about Bourbaki's army. Thus, Favre excluded the region where he was held up, near the Swiss border, from the armistice. The Government of National Defense still hoped that a miraculous victory by those forces could better their negotiating position. Instead, Bourbaki tried and failed to take his own life after facing numerous accusations over his leadership, and the army fell into disarray. Men were cold, hungry, and without equipment. Instead of fighting, they withdrew beyond the Swiss border on February 1st, factually ending the last flicker of the Franco-Prussian War.

Chapter 8 – Life Goes On: The Aftermath of the Franco-Prussian War

Though the armistice ended the fighting, factually finishing the war, it still had to legally be concluded through a peace treaty. That meant weeks of negotiations, with the French trying to stave off German thirst for vengeance.

The peace talks began in a much different balance of power than anyone in Europe had expected, including Bismarck and Moltke. France was at a low point that it hadn't seen for centuries, shamed by a disgraceful military defeat, a poor economy, and their land in ruins, not to mention the chaotic political scene. As agreed in the armistice, a nationwide election was held with the help of the Germans on February 8th. Unsurprisingly, the most successful were the candidates who promoted peace and liberty, so a majority of the seats in the National Assembly went to rural monarchists and conservatives, while the moderate republicans held less than 30 percent. Radical republicans even got votes, and surprisingly, there was also a handful of Bonapartists who gained seats. The new leader of what was now the French Third Republic was Adolphe Thiers, an old republican who helped to create the Second Republic in 1848. Thiers retained most of the ministers from the provisional government, including Favre. Gambetta, a continued proponent of the war, remained outside of it.

A legally constituted government gave Thiers legitimacy to negotiate with Bismarck, but the elections were far from being a soothing factor as some hoped. France remained deeply divided, with brewing discontent across all major cities. Like always, that feeling was strongest in Paris, where the working classes remained radical and prone to outbursts and riots. At the time, Bordeaux remained as the government headquarters, but Thiers wanted to regain control over the capital, which held to its anti-governmental sentiments. This led to a confrontation, sparked by the regular army trying to take a handful of obsolete guns left by the Prussians at the Parisian forts. On March 18th, the Paris Commune was established when the revolutionary Communards, as they called themselves, took control of the city once the army withdrew. This sparked similar but much less successful attempts to establish communes in other major cities, such as Lyon or Marseille. Regardless, the nation was entrenched in what can be characterized as a civil war. Such instability only worsened Thiers's negotiation position. It reduced his internal political strength as well as diplomatic reach, as it made most of the European monarchies quite wary of the Parisian radicals.

A barricade of the Paris Commune, preparing to defend their rebellion.
Source: https://commons.wikimedia.org/wiki/File:Barricade18March1871.jpg

Opposed to them stood the victorious and, more importantly, united Germany, just as Bismarck had planned. As he had expected and predicted, a defensive war against the French aroused nationalist feelings among the Germanic people. Nevertheless, Bismarck knew that he needed more than just public support, which, of course, wasn't spread equally among the independent Germanic states. On the one hand, Bavaria was the most opposed to the idea of unification, with such sentiments coming from a wider public as well as its ruler, King Ludwig II. On the other side of the spectrum, the Grand Duchy of Baden was wholly behind the idea, and it even petitioned to be admitted to the North German Confederation after 1866. Thus, as far back as September 1870, Bismarck had begun a series of talks and conferences with representatives from Bavaria, Baden, Hessen, and Württemberg. Through these, they agreed upon details of how these states would be incorporated into the newly formed German Confederation in November, creating the first step toward formal unification. These agreements were framed as more of federal agreements, with four independent Germanic countries retaining some sovereignty, for example, an independent post, railway, and army. Furthermore, it was an agreement between the North German Confederation and those states; thus, it didn't change the already existing relations between Prussia and the other already assimilated countries.

The next step was taken in the federal assembly, where in early December, a motion was proposed for reinstituting the German Empire and offering the imperial title to Prussian King Wilhelm I. To give this motion more strength, Bismarck arranged that it would be proposed by none other than Ludwig II. In fact, to secure his support, the chancellor arranged that the Bavarian king would be paid 300,000 marks annually from the so-called "Guelph Fund," a secretly seized Hanoverian state treasury that came into Prussian hands in 1866. It was nothing less than a bribe, and it remained a secret for a long time. Regardless, Bismarck continued his political machinations, and by January 1871, the proposed unification was put to the vote in the parliaments of the south Germanic states. As expected, the Bavarians were the most opposed, yet the decree was passed on January 21st, with a margin of only two votes.

A later rendition of the proclamation of the German Empire in the Hall of Mirrors at Versailles.
Source: https://commons.wikimedia.org/wiki/File:A_v_Werner_-Kaiserproklamation_am_18_Januar_1871_(3._Fassung_1885).jpg

However, Bismarck was sure the unification would be accepted; thus, on January 18th, he organized the official proclamation of the German Empire, or *Deutsches Kaiserreich*, sometimes also erroneously named the Second Reich. It was held in the Hall of Mirrors in Versailles, giving the event a double meaning. The date was the anniversary of when the Kingdom of Prussia was officially formed in 1701, and holding the entire ceremony in the most famous French palace was, of course, an exhibition of domination over their defeated enemies. It wasn't a grand ceremony, as most generals and officers showed up in their combat uniforms, and it was also riddled with problems for Bismarck. For example, Wilhelm wanted the title of Emperor of Germany, but his chancellor secured him the title of German Emperor, a title that Wilhelm thought had less grandeur and tradition. Regardless, the ceremony proceeded with everyone referring to him as simply Emperor or Kaiser Wilhelm. Bismarck saw this moment as his own crowning achievement, but accounts state that the overall atmosphere was cold and rather rigid, without a proper celebratory feel to it.

Despite the fact that most of the other European powers weren't too keen on the creation of a new empire in the heart of the continent, they did nothing to stop it. Shocked or impressed with the German victories over France, they deemed it unwise to interfere. With their internal and external positions so different, the French and the Germans began negotiating for peace on February 21st. The new empire was represented by Bismarck, while Thiers and Favre negotiated in the name of the French. The talks, held in Versailles, were tough and exhausting, especially for the Frenchmen. Bismarck demanded harsh terms, most notably the annexation of Alsace and Lorraine, but also an indemnity of six billion francs in gold. Those terms wouldn't just humiliate France; it would cripple the country. The reparations would be hard to pay on its own, but the two provinces the Germans demanded were also the industrial and economic heart of France, holding 20 percent of its mining and steel production potential.

Of course, Thiers tried to work around these issues, but Bismarck wouldn't budge much. This was partially caused by his own feelings toward the French. Furthermore, he believed that, unlike Austria, France would never forgive the Prussians for the victory, no matter how generous the peace terms were. Additionally, he had to account for political pressure. The masses in Germany more or less expected and demanded the annexation of these lands, while even Moltke, Roon, and even Wilhelm were also pressuring him to take as much as possible from the French. To them, it was punishment for all the spilled German blood, although Moltke was also thinking about the defensive needs in future wars. Thus, whenever Thiers tried to negotiate against the demands, Bismarck simply threatened him and France with the continuation of the war. On the other side, Favre and Thiers were aware that the French people would be unsatisfied with anything they could achieve in these talks, which were slowly turning into a dictation of terms. Ultimately, they could do little to sway Bismarck.

When it came to the matter of ceding territories, from the German point of view, the question wasn't "if" but "how much." During the negotiations, there were several contested issues. Roon advocated for annexation all the way to Nancy, yet Bismarck didn't press that far. However, when he considered giving up on Metz, Moltke and other officers were outraged. Initially, Bismarck didn't consider Metz as incredibly valuable, arguing that he would rather take more money and build a new fort a few miles away from it. Yet, the German military personnel were adamant, so he was forced to pressure the French for it. Then they focused on Belfort, which was too much for Thiers. After further arguments, the chancellor said he would consult Wilhelm and Moltke. In the end, it all came down to Moltke's decision, and the field marshal was prepared to back down from Belfort if Thiers would give up four less important villages in Lorraine, which had ten thousand buried Prussians. He also demanded a military entrance and victory parade in Paris. Thiers accepted, as long as the French could retain an important fort, in exchange for this humiliation in the capital.

A photograph of the German victory parade in Paris.
Source: *https://commons.wikimedia.org/wiki/File:Prussians_parade_thru_Paris_March_1871.jpg*

There were also a lot of negotiations around the indemnity. Thiers initially offered 1.5 billion francs, but Bismarck refused. He wanted more, not only to embarrass the French and get back at them for humiliations in the previous century or so but also to impede their ability to seek retribution. In the end, Bismarck agreed to lower the indemnity to no less than five billion francs to be paid off by 1875. To put it in some perspective, this amounted to about 23 percent of the French annual GDP at the time or around two and a half times the annual government budget. Thiers had no more room for haggling and had to accept. Many foreign observers were shocked and appalled by these reparations, as they went beyond covering the expenses of the war. Some claimed that this could be a dangerous precedent, as it could mean wars might be fought for pure monetary gain. Furthermore, France had to bear a lighter form of German occupation until the indemnity was paid off in full.

Finally, France had to recognize the German unification, the proclamation of the empire, and Wilhelm I as the emperor. This proved to be of little concern to the French when compared to other issues. Apart from that, the two sides agreed upon some technical matters, like the framework of withdrawing from certain regions or forms of payments. Since Bismarck was in a hurry to finish the whole ordeal to focus on building a newly unified nation, he pressured Thiers to accept the peace treaty immediately. Thus, on February 26th, a preliminary peace was signed, but it still had to be ratified by two governments. On March 1st, thirty thousand German troops entered the city, parading for their emperor to the disgust of the Parisians. However, the French government in Bordeaux signed the peace treaty the same day, preventing any further parades. This came as a surprise to the Germans, who expected them to have a lengthy debate in the National Assembly. Thus, by March 3rd, the German troops had evacuated from Paris, though sizable armies remained in the vicinity as part of the occupation force. In Berlin, the newly formed Reichstag, the German assembly, accepted the treaty on March 21st. The formal signing of the agreement was held in Frankfurt on May 10th, formally ending the war between France and Germany.

By then, Thiers was already more concerned with the Paris Commune, which took over control of the capital. Luckily for the French government, the Germans were as hostile to the Communards as they were. Bismarck may have reveled in the glorious mess that France had become, but he saw radical republicanism and emerging communism as a threat to everyone. Thus, he actually went on to provide undirect assistance to France. First, he agreed to allow the French to send eighty thousand troops north of the Loire, which wasn't allowed by the peace treaty. Then, he expedited the release of prisoners, seeking to build up the strength of the French Army to allow it to retake its own capital. Apart from that, they refrained from interfering, as it was a rather delicate issue. Nonetheless, they served as a blockade to the Communards, as their lines near Paris were closed to any movements from or to the city. Thanks to this, the French Army, with more than 100,000 men, led by the recently released MacMahon, entered the capital on May 21st. Fighting ensued, but some thirty thousand armed revolutionaries were defeated by May 28th, ending the first communist experiment in history to the relief of many, including Bismarck.

With that, peace was finally restored in Europe, at least for a while. On the German side, there were about twenty-eight thousand killed in action and some ninety thousand wounded. Additionally, diseases reportedly took some 12,000 more lives from the German ranks, totaling some 130,000 casualties overall. The French paid for their struggle much more steeply. They had roughly 140,000 dead, with about 45,000 succumbing to various diseases. Furthermore, they had about the same number of wounded, raising their total to roughly 280,000 casualties. On top of that, they had more than 380,000 men imprisoned in Germany, with an additional 95,000 in Switzerland and Belgium; these men had crossed the border to escape the war. These men were, of course, released in the weeks and months after the treaty was signed. On top of that, French civilian casualties should be added; however, there are no clear numbers for them. There are estimates of about twenty thousand civilians losing their lives during the Paris Commune, but the exact number of people during the clash with the Germans is unclear. The initial French reports of civilian casualties put the number at around two thousand or slightly more. However, these seem to be victims of direct military actions, for example, the bombardment of Paris, and excludes people dying from starvation and similar byproducts of war. In reality, French civilian casualties may go up to anywhere between 80,000 to 100,000.

A map of Europe in 1871 with the nations' new borders. The shaded part of France was under temporary German occupation.

Regardless of the losses, both nations had pressing issues to deal with as the dust of the war settled. France was politically fractured, economically devastated, and also suffered from the partial German occupation. To finally liberate itself from the last lingering pressures of the defeat, France strained its finances and paid off the indemnity by September 1873, two years before its due date, ending German military presence on its soil. Despite that, the loss of Alsace and

Lorraine remained an issue for many in France. The French economy was slow to recover, as it lost its most vital industrial zones to the Germans, but it managed to get back on its feet in the upcoming years and decades, not without the help of France's vast colonial empire. However, French politics remained somewhat unstable for a long time, as there were many parties, including several monarchists. The Third Republic, as it was called, remained in provisional form until 1875, when a series of laws allowed for the formation of a constitution. With these laws, the government was divided into a two-house legislative system, with both a premier and a president of the republic. Despite that, French politics remained turbulent.

Despite the victory, the newly formed German Empire also had a lot of issues to deal with, especially from Bismarck's perspective. Despite the unification, the new nation was built on a rather unstable federal organization, something that Bismarck worked hard to rectify. Although this never actually changed from a constitutional perspective, the chancellor began equating the laws through several legislative codices. He simultaneously worked on national unity through forced Germanization. This added another bonding factor among the German people in the empire, but it proved to be more than damaging to minorities, like the French in the west, the Danes in the north, and the Poles in the east. On the political scene, Germany proved somewhat stable for a while, with Wilhelm and Bismarck at its helm, but there were plenty of struggles between the various parties. Religious issues were part of these political turbulences, as the Catholic south struggled with the Protestant north. In terms of the economy, Germany flourished due to its rapid industrialization and expanding railways, helped both by the indemnity and acquisition of Alsace and Lorraine. In the years after the war, the German Empire became second only to Great Britain in regards to the greatest economy in Europe, and it was in competition with the United States for the title of world's second-best economy.

As for the leading people of the Franco-Prussian War, they had varying fates. The Bonapartes remained in Great Britain. Napoleon III died a broken man in exile in 1873. His son, Napoleon IV, tried to prove his mettle in war and built up his political credibility. Yet, he lost his life in 1879 in the Zulu War. Thiers remained in office until 1873, but he remained politically present until his death in 1877. He was succeeded by none other than MacMahon, who acted as the French president until 1879. Afterward, he quietly retired from politics. Bazaine was put on trial for treason and convicted to life in prison in 1873, but he escaped to Spain, where he spent his last days. Favre's political career was finished as far back as 1871 when a series of scandals regarding his children from illicit affairs brought him down. Finally, Gambetta continued to play an active political role, serving as the minister of the interior and a premier before he died in an accident in 1882.

On the German side, Emperor Wilhelm I remained on the throne until his death in 1888. Despite vast constitutional power, he remained largely in Bismarck's shadow. Bismarck remained the chancellor of the empire while also serving as a foreign minister and a prime minister of Prussia until 1890, controlling most of German politics until then. He resigned only after clashing with the new emperor, Wilhelm's grandson of the same name, Wilhelm II. Moltke remained the chief of the General Staff until he resigned in 1888, and he then served as a member of the Reichstag until his death in 1891. Roon played several political and military roles immediately after the war, but due to his poor health, he retired quickly afterward, dying in 1879. All three of them were awarded titles after their victory over the French. Moltke and Roon were named counts (*Graf*), while Bismarck was given a princely title (*Fürst*).

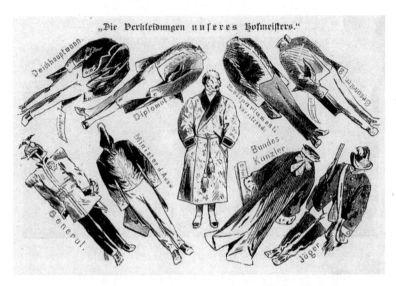

A caricature depicting Bismarck choosing suits for many of his roles in German politics.
Source: https://commons.wikimedia.org/wiki/File:Httpdigi.ub.uni-heidelberg.dediglitklabismarck18900050a.jpg

Thus, by the end of the century, most of the major actors of the war were gone. However, the legacy of the conflict outlasted them, proving to be one of the major events in modern history. Its consequences would certainly be felt by future generations.

Epilogue

The Franco-Prussian War and the peace treaty that ended it proved to be rather controversial, both to their contemporaries and for future politicians and historians. For those observing it, it was a shocking event. It marked a fall of a major power and the birth of another. Furthermore, the peace treaty was seen as one of the harshest in recent history, both in terms of indemnity and territorial losses. On the French side, it birthed revanchism, as the people felt the need to resettle the score with the Germans. On the other side, the Germans began feeling superior, demanding recognition and a place among the world superpowers. Contemporaries also judged that the Franco-Prussian conflict caused a major rebalancing of power in Europe and the world.

The tensions between Germany and France prevailed for decades, and a number of alliances formed around this animosity. Initially, the German Empire, under Bismarck's guidance, proved more adept at this diplomatic game. He organized a pact with two other European empires—Russia and Austria—to prevent the two from joining forces with France to curb the rising power of Germany. He also sought to avoid irritating Britain, which cared little who was dominating the continent as long as it didn't jeopardize the British colonial empire. With France isolated, Europe remained somewhat peaceful.

However, things began to change in the 1880s, as Germany's economic advance began to worry others. Furthermore, the youngest European empire also wanted a place among the colonial powers, joining the infamous Scramble for Africa. Britain took notice of this. Things only took a turn for the worse when Bismarck and Wilhelm I exited the political stage in Germany. The new generation of politicians, led by Emperor Wilhelm II, became increasingly aggressive in their stance. France took this opportunity to ally itself with Britain and Russia, which had changed sides after its pact with Germany expired. On the other side stood Austria, Italy, and the German Empire. All three nations sought to expand their positions on the world stage. The platform was set for the Great War, which would explode in 1914.

This causational link between 1870 and 1914 led many historians and politicians to speculate that one of the major causes for World War I was the harsh treaty imposed on the French, most notably the loss of Alsace and Lorraine. Though there are some truths to this sentiment, as many in France were itching to regain the lost lands, it would be too simplistic a view of the whole situation. It loses track of the longstanding animosity between the two nations while ignoring the fact that the most impactful result of the Franco-Prussian War was the European power system being thrown out of balance.

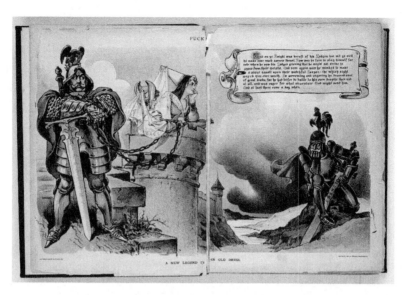

A caricature depicting the French yearning to liberate Alsace and Lorraine.
Source: https://commons.wikimedia.org/wiki/File:A_new_legend_in_an_old_dress_-_Keppler._LCCN2012647516.jpg

Nevertheless, all these consequences of the war are circumstantial, as other factors contributed to it as well. The only legacy solely linked to it was the reform of how the militaries functioned. The entire world was fascinated with Germany's success and decided to copy it to some degree. While some tried to reproduce it to the tiniest tactical detail, like, for example, Russia against the Ottoman Empire in 1878, most were more focused on the grand scale. By 1914, the entire world, from Washington to Tokyo, adopted Moltke's standing General Staff, widespread conscription, rapid and organized mobilization, the use of railways for supply and deployment, a focus on artillery, and the division of the army into smaller, more mobile and interchangeable units. All of these were to become hallmarks of the Great War, at least partially.

However, the imitators and even German successors failed to realize that Moltke's military genius wasn't an independent entity. Most of them neglected the brilliance of Bismarck's politics, and they were unable to recognize that the great German success of 1870 was achieved through a rather turbulent but fruitful partnership between two remarkable persons, who led a motivated and bustling nation in conditions that were perfect for them. Such shortsightedness of later generations led to no less than two major world wars, which, in a simplified view, were essentially an attempt to replicate the Franco-Prussian War on a grander scale. Other nations fared similarly when trying to replicate German success in their confrontations with France.

Conclusion

A short war, like the one fought by the French and the Prussians in 1870, is rarely so impactful in history. Yet the Franco-Prussian War proved to be a turning point in European and world history. It led to a rise of an empire, new military technologies and strategies, and the birth of the "total war" mentality of conflicts. It created more tensions than it solved, such as the first steps toward later major wars. As such, the Franco-Prussian conflict deserves to be studied, as it holds important lessons in military, diplomatic, and political action and thought.

However, instead of trying to learn how to wage war, like many before us did, it is vital to look at this war as a warning. It showcases what happens when nationalism and personal political ambitions leads us forward, as it brings unnecessary conflicts, destruction, and death. The war between France and Prussia was ultimately avoidable, as it was caused by politicians and rulers who didn't see the battlefield, leaving the fighting and dying to the people they were supposedly representing and leading. Worst of all, it only led to the continued circle of vicious violence. That circle was only broken when French and German leaders after World War II decided there was too much death and destruction, not to mention the shame they felt in participating in such events. Thus, it would be much better if we would be able to sense that shame before straying into ultimately futile conflicts.

Lessons of peace are some of the most important that can be taught by history, and hopefully, this guide managed to convey similar sentiments. Yet, reading this shouldn't be an end but rather just a beginning of your curious exploration of the human past, both of this particular topic but also in other areas of history. Let us all learn from the mistakes of the people who came before us, lest we repeat them again.

Here's another book by Captivating History that you might like

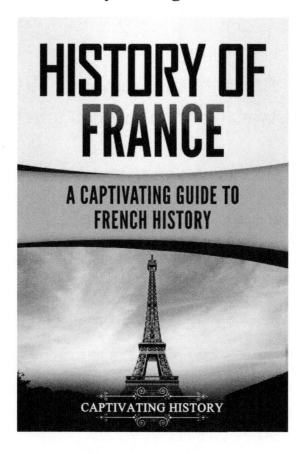

Free Bonus from Captivating History
(Available for a Limited time)

Hi History Lovers!

Now you have a chance to join our exclusive history list so you can get your first history ebook for free as well as discounts and a potential to get more history books for free! Simply visit the link below to join.

Captivatinghistory.com/ebook

Also, make sure to follow us on Facebook, Twitter and Youtube by searching for Captivating History.

Bibliography

Geoffrey Wawro, *The Franco-Prussian War: The German Conquest of France in 1870–1871*, Cambridge University Press, 2003.

Quintin Barry, *The Franco-Prussian War 1870-71 - Volumes 1 & 2*, Helion & Company, 2007.

Stephen Badsey, *The Franco-Prussian War 1870-1871*, 2003.

Michael Howard, *The Franco-Prussian War: The German Invasion of France 1870–1871*, Routledge, 2001.

Jason Philip Coy, *A Brief History of Germany*, Facts on File, 2011.

A, Farmer and A. Stiles, *The Unification of Germany 1815–1919*, Hodder Education, 2007.

Jonathan Steinberg, *Bismarck: A Life*, Oxford University Press, 2011.

Malcolm Crook, *Revolutionary France 1788–1880*, Oxford University Press, 2002.

Melville D. Landon, *The Franco-Prussian War in a Nutshell - A Daily Diary of Diplomacy, Battles, and War Literature*, G. W. Cakleton & Co., 1871.

Michael A. Palmer, *The German War: A Concise History 1859-1945*, Zenith Press, 2010.

H. Hearder, *Europe in the Nineteenth Century 1830-1880*, Longman, 1966.

Robert Gerwarth, *The Bismarck Myth - Weimar Germany and the Legacy of the Iron Chancellor*, Oxford University Press, 2005.

James Retallack, *Imperial Germany 1871–1918*, Oxford University Press, 2008.

Stefan Berger, *A Companion to Nineteenth-Century Europe 1789–1914*, Blackwell Publishing, 2006.

Dennis Showalter, *The wars of German unification*, Bloomsbury academic, 2015.

Otto Pflanze, *Bismarck and the Development of Germany – The Period of Unification 1815-1871*, Princeton University Press, 1963.

A. J. P. Taylor, *Bismarck: The Man and the Statesman*, Vintage Books, 1967.

Count Helmuth Von Moltke, *The Franco-German War of 1870-71*, The Project Gutenberg EBook, 2011 (Originally: James R. Osgood, McIlvaine & CO. 1893).

Micheal Clodfelter, *Warfare and Armed Conflicts: A Statistical Encyclopedia of Casualty and Other Figures, 1492-2015*, McFarland, 2017.